# AFTA SpringerBriefs in Family Therapy

**A Publication of the American Family Therapy Academy**

Founded in 1977, the **American Family Therapy Academy** is a non-profit organization of leading family therapy teachers, clinicians, program directors, policymakers, researchers, and social scientists dedicated to advancing systemic thinking and practices for families in their social context.

**Vision**

AFTA envisions a just world by transforming social contexts that promote health, safety, and well-being of all families and communities.

**Mission**

AFTA's mission is developing, researching, teaching, and disseminating progressive, just family therapy and family-centered practices and policies.

More information about this series at http://www.springer.com/series/11846

Victoria Dickerson
Editor

# Poststructural and Narrative Thinking in Family Therapy

AFTA
American Family Therapy Academy

Springer

*Editor*
Victoria Dickerson
Aptos, CA
USA

ISSN 2196-5528 ISSN 2196-5536 (electronic)
AFTA SpringerBriefs in Family Therapy
ISBN 978-3-319-31488-4 ISBN 978-3-319-31490-7 (eBook)
DOI 10.1007/978-3-319-31490-7

Library of Congress Control Number: 2016936280



Printed on acid-free paper

This Springer imprint is published by Springer Nature
The registered company is Springer International Publishing AG Switzerland

# Foreword

The *AFTA SpringerBriefs in Family Therapy* is an official publication of the American Family Therapy Academy. Each volume focuses on the practice and policy implications of innovative systemic research and theory in family therapy and allied fields. Our goal is to make information about families and systemic practices in societal contexts widely accessible in a reader-friendly, conversational, and practical style. We have asked the authors to make their personal context, location, and experience visible in their writing. AFTA's core commitment to equality, social responsibility, and justice are represented in each volume.

Vicki Dickerson has edited a volume that makes complex theoretical ideas associated with poststructural thinking and narrative therapy alive and personal. The authors help readers see the effects of dominant cultural discourses in people's lives and share richly detailed examples of the creative and innovative ways they apply narrative principles in family therapy. They invite us to reflect on the nuances of practice; how therapists can be influential while privileging client preferences and values, how to bear witness, remember, and structure questions that help clients notice what is possible and craft the alternative stories they prefer.

I hope you enjoy these chapters as much as I did. I especially appreciate the generosity of the authors in making their thinking and practices so visible and accessible and thank them for stimulating my deep appreciation for the transformative power of narrative work.

Portland, OR

Carmen Knudson-Martin
Series Editor
Lewis & Clark College

# Acknowledgments

This book began as an inspiration drawn on a series of presentations at the Therapeutic Conversations Conference in Vancouver, Canada, in 2014. It occurred to me that the offerings I encountered there could benefit from a wider audience. Thus was set in motion an invitation to several of my colleagues and friends to communicate their remarkable work in writing. This *SpringerBrief* is one outcome of that endeavor.

I am continually grateful to AFTA for being my professional home for over 20 years. I am likewise appreciative of my narrative community, many of whom are also AFTA members. In both groups, I have found others who share my philosophy and values, colleagues who have become friends, persons I would otherwise not have known. The values we all hold dear include a commitment to social justice, a belief in the possibilities of change for and investment in families, and a direction toward bettering the field of family therapy.

Thanks then, of course, to the authors of this book on *Poststructural and Narrative Thinking in Family Therapy*. The material is original and published here for the first time. The authors are all practicing clinicians and teachers of narrative therapy. How fortunate we are to have them share their ideas and their experience with us.

# Contents

# Editor and Contributors

## About the Editor

**Victoria Dickerson Ph.D.** has been involved with narrative ideas for over 25 years and has been active in writing numerous articles, book chapters, and two books in that period of time. She is active with the American Family Therapy Academy, having been Vice-President, board member, and committee chair over the past 20 years. She has a private practice and is the Social Media/Communications Strategist for the Family Process Institute. She lives in Aptos, California with her dog Rio and her cat Tigresa. She is the editor of this *SpringerBrief* and recently also edited a special section on narrative and poststructural ideas for the journal *Family Process*.

## Contributors

**Kathie Crocket Ph.D.** is Associate Professor and the Director of Counsellor Education at the University of Waikato. She teaches professional practice—in particular narrative approaches to therapy—in the M.Couns program, and supervises master's and doctoral research in counseling. Her current research emphases are research supervision, school guidance counseling, professional ethics, and professional supervision.

**Stephen Gaddis Ph.D.** is the Founder and Director of the Narrative Therapy Initiative in Salem, Massachusetts. He has worked as a narrative therapist for over 20 years. He graduated from the second International Training Program at the Dulwich Centre in 2005 and has taught narrative therapy in New Zealand, South Africa, Norway, and Canada, as well as around the U.S. He has published papers on narrative therapy nationally and internationally, and is currently working on his first book. He lives in Marblehead, Massachusetts where he has the privilege of sharing a life with Ashley, his wife, and their children, Will and Laurel.

**Lorraine Hedtke MSW, LCSW, Ph.D.** teaches about death, dying, and bereavement throughout the U.S. and internationally. Her unique ideas and practices can be found in her books about grief that represents a departure from the conventional models of grief psychology. She is Professor and Program Coordinator of a Graduate Counseling program at California State University San Bernardino. She also is the Founder of The Fabula Center, a counseling and training center, is a faculty member of the Vancouver School of Narrative Therapy, and is Associate of the Taos Institute.

**Elmarie Kotzé D Litt et Phil.** teaches in the Counsellor Education Programme, Te Oranga Human Development and Movement Studies, University of Waikato in Aotearoa New Zealand. She supervises doctoral candidates' and M Couns students' research projects. She has co-authored several articles and book chapters with colleagues, graduates, and students.

**Andrew Kulasingham MCS, MCouns (Hons)** is Head of Counselling at ImpacTauranga, a local community agency in Tauranga, New Zealand, working with young people and their families. He is also on the faculty of Faith Bible College, NZ, where he teaches theology. He is married to his best friend, Rhena, and they are proud parents of three amazing young adults.

**Colin James Sanders Ph.D.** has taught with the Master of Counselling Program with City University of Seattle in Vancouver, Canada, since 1998, and currently is Director of the British Columbia Master of Counselling Program. Colin taught with the Vancouver School of Narrative Therapy (VSNT) from 1993 to 2013. Colin has written several book chapters, journal articles, and a dissertation relating to his theoretical perspectives and therapeutic practices over the years, in addition to articles and interviews pertaining to poetry and poetics. He lives on B.C.'s "Sunshine Coast" with his partner Gail, and their two cats. Gail and Colin have three grandsons, with Colin's children, Maya and Adrian.

**John Stillman LCSW** is a co-founder and clinical social worker at Caspersen Therapy and Training Center in St. Louis Park, Minnesota, where he practices narrative therapy with children, adolescents, and adults. As Director of Caspersen Training Center, he provides narrative therapy training to professionals from multiple disciplines. In 2002, he was a member of the first diplomate program taught by Michael White at the Dulwich Centre in Adelaide, Australia, and is an international narrative therapy trainer. He lives in Minneapolis, Minnesota, with his wife and two sons, and dog, and raises chickens and keeps bees.

# What Is Narrative Therapy? Poststructural and Narrative Thinking in Family Therapy Practice

**Victoria Dickerson**

**Abstract** The introductory chapter to this book on "Poststructural and Narrative Thinking in Family Therapy Practice" gives a brief description of narrative therapy as well as a rendition of what has become possible in the furthering of narrative ideas and practices. The work of narrative theorists and practitioners has a wide reach from the Southern Hemisphere to countries across the globe; the selections in this book not only emphasize concepts that originated with Michael White but also expand his thinking to new possibilities. The emphasis on meaning, positioning, and understanding problems as created by a cultural understanding cuts across all the chapters. It may seem that a therapist may not have a solid foot on which to stand, but then, no one really does. So, from a narrative/poststructural perspective, the work is to co-create an agreed upon place to co-research possibilities for future-preferred performances—a stance of both protest and wonder.

## Introduction

Inevitably the question arises how a movement would have progressed if the creator had lived or had continued on as its leader. The passing of Michael White unexpectedly in 2008 left many of those outside of the narrative therapy community raising that question. There were predictions that his innovative approach would lose momentum and lack the creativity and continuous development that Michael brought to the work. Michael's voracious reading and ongoing adaptation of the narrative metaphor invigorated it and all those who were learning and teaching and putting his ideas into practice (Denborough 2009). Would that kind of dedication and passion continue when his presence was no longer among us?

In the numerous psychologies that have come before—Freud, Jung, Rogers, Beck, to name a few—the work they originated has continued and morphed to a number of viable approaches and integrative therapies. Does the narrative metaphor

V. Dickerson (✉)
Aptos and Los Gatos, CA, USA
e-mail: vcd@cruzio.com



V. Dickerson (ed.), *Poststructural and Narrative Thinking in Family Therapy*,
AFTA SpringerBriefs in Family Therapy, DOI 10.1007/978-3-319-31490-7_1

belong in the ranks of the greats? Michael never particularly thought of himself as a "guru" or the only one in the narrative community with new ideas; he did acknowledge that, along with David Epston, he was the "originator" of a special "brand" of therapy (White and Epston 1990). He situated his thinking and his work in the center of a poststructural epistemology, drawing on Foucault, Derrida, Vygotsgy, and others within this burgeoning philosophical position (see Dickerson 2009, 2010).

From a different tradition, one of production and management, we have other founders who have left their organizations (or movements) and passed on their leadership. Steve Jobs with Apple is an example; he left, and when he returned, he revitalized the organization. After his death in 2011, his leadership fell to the chief operating officer Tim Cook. Howard Schultz bought Starbucks in 1987 from the original founders but then left in 2000; when he returned in 2008, he reinvented the company to fit more closely with his initial vision. Bill Gates with Microsoft passed the baton in 2000 to Steve Ballmer, who more recently in 2014 left the position of CEO to Satya Nadella. All of these transitions have led to mixed results.

In any case, might we expect that things would continue in the same vein? Perhaps we could hope that those who followed would sustain the original vision, although the performance may take on many different permutations. What then has occurred within the continuance of the narrative approach?

Michael White's leaving was unpredicted; however in the eight years since Michael's passing, there are many who follow his thinking and practice, those who have taken up the torch. A special section in the September 2009 issue of *Family Process* (Dickerson 2009) entitled "Drawing Inspiration from the Legacy of Michael White" makes the case for a rich continuation of narrative ideas as practiced by a large number of narrative therapists following Michael's profound vision. Therapeutic Conversations, a conference organized by Stephen Madigan (more recently along with David Epston), has a long history of inviting new thinking and continually reimagining Michael's ideas.

## What Is Narrative Therapy?

Is there a straightforward way to summarize the narrative metaphor that Michael initiated? At the risk of "thinning" this very rich approach to understanding persons, problems, and change, the following is an attempt at an appreciation of this epistemology.

Michael White was averse to the idea that problems existed in people or that in any way persons were deficient. The deficit understanding of individualizing psychologies was anathema to him. The same is true of his appreciation of families; the pathologizing of families as dysfunctional seemed unkind and misrepresentative of what was possible in relationships. Michael, instead, saw problems as an effect of larger cultural grand narratives (discourses) about how people were supposed to be and act, as these narratives offered taken-for-granted meanings that were unchallenged and therefore considered as "truth." When persons had experiences and attributed meaning to those experiences, the meanings available to them resided in those very cultural narratives. Thus, as persons storied their experience, they often considered themselves "problematized," outside of what was deemed appropriate or correct.

Michael's reading of Foucault (1972, 1980) led to his particular understandings of these dominant, and often subjugating, discourses and thus the need to "de-construct" those narratives. This process could often make visible what were seen as "exceptions," "unique outcomes," or possibilities that were more preferred. As Michael began to incorporate Derrida's (1978, 1981) thinking in his writing, he developed an appreciation of what he called the "absent but implicit," possibilities and preferences, often unnoticed or on the other side of what is presented as a problem story.

My belief is that no understanding of a narrative approach can occur without embracing this cultural cornerstone. Processes of deconstructing, noticing exceptions or the absent but implicit, having a de-centered but influential stance, and co-constructing preferred performances of life are all therapeutic practices made possible by a central positioning: an appreciation of the effects of cultural discourse. (See Madigan (2010) for a much richer and detailed exposition of narrative therapy.)

## What Follows

In this *Springer Brief* on "Poststructural and Narrative Thinking in Family Therapy," we see specific evidence of the growth of the narrative metaphor and its influence on the field of family therapy (Dickerson 2014; Dickerson also edited a special section on "New Ideas and Practices in Narrative Therapy" in the June 2016 issue of *Family Process*). One can easily notice the brilliant effects of the maturation of narrative ideas across a variety of thinkers and practitioners in a range of geographical settings. The offerings range from detailed and thickened expositions of key ideas in Michael's original work (e.g., "de-centered and influential," "re-membering practices," and "autoethnography") to an extension of his intentions in "aesthetics of engagement" to an organization of his ideas into key "principles." The geographical scope extends from Canada to New Zealand, California to Massachusetts to Minnesota. Although narrative ideas and practices have taken shape and form in Israel, South America, Africa, China, and among other countries and continents, these authors hail from English-speaking countries and share a wide assortment of understandings.

The initial chapter (after this introduction) by Stephen Gaddis is a rich clinical example of Michael's key therapeutic concept "De-centered and Influential." You will also find an excellent rendering of narrative theory—another version of my summary above.

I met Steve in Vancouver in the mid-1990s at a Narrative Conference organized by Stephen Madigan. Steve was a graduate student at the time and I found myself excited by his enthusiasm for the ideas. He went on to be a visiting teaching fellow for a year in the early 2000s at the University of Waikato in Hamilton, New Zealand, where he worked with Kathie Crocket and Elmarie Kotzé (two of the co-authors of the next chapter in this book). Currently, Steve runs his own narrative training institute in Salem, Massachusetts (see http://www.narrativetherapyinitiative.org/).

In this chapter, Steve takes the reader inside a thickly described clinical example. This will likely open the door to a clearer understanding of what it means for a therapist to take a de-centered and influential position. Hopefully, this knowledge can enrich the reader's own clinical practice.

The chapter following is by Elmarie Kotzé, Andrew Kulasingham, and Kathie Crocket. The threads of a way of thinking expressed by Deleuze and Guattari run through this chapter aptly titled "Reimagining Family" as it illustrates the use of an autoethnography. Just prior to his death Michael had been reading Deleuze, and some narrative theorists have further explored his ideas (see Winslade 2009, and Hedtke, this issue). This chapter also describes "re-membering practices," central to the chapter by Hedtke that follows.

Elmarie is currently a senior lecturer in the counseling program at the University of Waikato, mentioned above, where Kathie is the director; Andrew was recently a student there. The counseling program at that university is steeped in a teaching/learning tradition of narrative ideas and practices from the late 1990s (see Monk et al. 1997). I met both Elmarie and Kathie in 1999 at a Narrative Conference in Adelaide, Australia, and have been privileged to continue a friendship with them ever since. Kathie and I have also co-authored a book chapter (Dickerson & Crocket 2010) entitled "El Tigre, El Tigre: A Story of Narrative Practice"—a generative and generous collaboration.

The autoethnography described here opens to the reader an understanding of how the therapist can use one's personal experience within the weave of a clinical connection. I imagine the reader will resonate with much of the clinical story told here and find it useful in her/his own practice.

"Matrilineal Connections" is the title of the next chapter in which the author Lorraine Hedtke speaks in detail of "remembering conversations" or the "re-membering practices" referred to above. Lorraine has taken this very special concept that Michael developed based on Myerhoff's (1978) work with an aging Jewish community in Venice, California. Lorraine's thickening of these ideas is richly described in her detailed description of a clinical example with a woman whose mother has just died.

Although I met Lorraine in 1999 at the same conference in Australia mentioned above, it was not until fairly recently, 2014, that we became reacquainted. I was delighted to sit in on her presentation at a Therapeutic Conversations conference in Vancouver and learn of her in depth work with remembering conversations. She on her own, and also with her partner, John Winslade, has written about these ideas in other places (see Lorraine's chapter for references).

I am pleased to have her most recent update in this book. I suspect the reader will find this approach very helpful in his/her own clinical work with persons who have lost a loved one.

The following chapter by Colin Sanders describes an "Aesthetics of Engagement," drawing primarily from the work of Levinas and reprising Colin's recent doctoral dissertation as well. Colin aptly draws from multiple knowledges and voices and intricately interweaves these into a coherent understanding of how we, as therapists, engage our clients. His own rich experience as a clinician stands out as exemplar for this chapter.

I have likely known Colin the longest, meeting him at one of the first Narrative Conferences in the early 1990s; our lives have intertwined through the years as we catch up as often as we can on our work and our thinking. Colin's extensive reading includes anthropology and literature, and it is from this backdrop that he has made major contributions to narrative thinking over the years. I have used Colin's excellent writing (Sanders 1998, 2007) on addiction and substance misuse in my teaching over time. It is a pleasure to have his chapter here.

Lastly, we have John Stillman's organization of major narrative concepts into "Narrative Therapy Principles" and the use of vignettes to illustrate their usefulness. I met John at an AFTA Conference in 2011, where, along with Michael Unger, we invited John to present for us at the interest group on "Evaluating Poststructural Therapies." John Stillman's efforts at teaching narrative therapy as a set of principles have wide application, as you will read in his chapter and in his on-site and online training program (see http://www.caspersentrainingcenter.com/home/). He addresses a continuing dilemma: how to make complex ideas available to a wide population without diluting the rich epistemology on which the ideas are based (see Dickerson 2010).

John is the author of *Narrative Therapy Trauma Manual* (Stillman 2010), where he first began the process of organizing narrative ideas into "principles" in an effort to manualize the narrative approach—a formidable task. In an era of evidence-based practices, there continues to be attempts to create such a base for a poststructural approach—narrative therapy. However, these are quixotic at best.

As Kathie Crocket writes in a (Crocket 2008) book chapter: "Narrative therapy is philosophically at odds with the principles that produce nomothetic studies" (p. 523). After six years of my leading the AFTA interest group on "Evaluating Poststructural Therapies," I have become aware of numerous attempts worldwide. There does seem to have been some headway in research that shows a narrative approach as evidence-based (see http://dulwichcentre.com.au/narrative-therapy-research/). The caveat is that it is difficult to use a "structural" project—randomized clinical trial research—to measure a "poststructural" therapeutic endeavor.

Perhaps John's distillation of complex concepts into principles is paving the way to a more measurable course of action.

## Conclusion

You, as the reader of this special *Springer Brief* on "Poststructural and Narrative Thinking in Family Therapy Practice," can make your own decision about how to understand and digest the complexity offered here. Does the concept of "aesthetics of engagement" and all that this notion entails in the therapist–client relationship appeal to you? Or are you more drawn to thickened descriptions and rich clinical examples of some of Michael's initiatives (de-centered and influential, autoethnography, remembering practices) as developed further in these chapters? Or do your lean toward a grasp of principles organized around key concepts and how they are employed in teaching situations? Wherever your appreciation takes you, we, the authors, hope that these writings can enrich your clinical understandings and enhance the experience of those who meet with you for assistance.

As I have written previously, "A poststructural stance is about questioning and wondering; it is not about having answers, nor understanding everything. It is also a viewpoint that is a protest against normative ways of thinking, focused on appreciating people, families, and couples as experts in their own lives, intent on cocreating alternative ways of being and living, and committed to social justice" (Dickerson 2014, p. 412).

## References

Crocket, K. (2008). Narrative therapy. In J. Frew & M. D. Spiegler (Eds.), *Contemporary therapies for a diverse world* (pp. 489–531). New York: Houghton Mifflin.

Denborough, D. (2009). Some reflections on the legacies of Michael White: An Australian perspective. *The Australian and New Zealand Journal of Family Therapy, 30*, 92–108.

Derrida, J. (1978). *Writing and difference* (A. Bass, Trans.). Chicago: University of Chicago Press.

Derrida, J. (1981). *Positions*. Chicago: University of Chicago Press.

Dickerson, V. C. (2009). Introduction to the special section—Continuing narrative ideas and practices: Drawing inspiration from the legacy of Michael White. *Family Process, 48*, 315–318.

Dickerson, V. C. (2010). Positioning oneself within an epistemology: Refining our thinking about integrative approaches. *Family Process, 49*, 349–368.

Dickerson, V. C. (2014). The advance of poststructuralism and its influence on family therapy. *Family Process, 53*, 401–414.

Dickerson, V. C., & Crocket, K. (2010). "El Tigre," "El Tigre": A story of narrative practice. In A. Gurman (Ed.), *Clinical casebook of couple therapy* (pp. 153–180). New York: Guilford Press.

Foucault, M. (1972). *The archeology of knowledge*. London: Tavistock.

Foucault, M. (1980). *Power/knowledge: Selected interviews and other writings*. New York: Pantheon Books.

Madigan, S. (2010). *Narrative therapy: Theory and practice*. Chicago: American Psychology Association Press.

Myerhoff, B. (1978). *Number our days*. New York, NY: Simon & Schuster.

Monk, G., Winslade, J., Crocket, K., & Epston, D. (1997). *Narrative therapy in practice: The archaeology of hope*. San Francisco: Jossey-Bass Publishers.

Sanders, C. (1998). Substance misuse dilemmas: A postmodern inquiry. In S. Madigan & I. Law (Eds.), *Praxis: Situating discourse, feminism, and politics in narrative therapies* (pp. 141–162). Vancouver, Canada: Yaletown Family Therapy/Cardigan Press.
Sanders, C. (2007). A poetics of resistance: Compassionate practice in substance misuse therapy. In C. Brown & T. Augusta-Scott (Eds.), *Narrative therapy: Making meaning, making lives* (pp. 59–76). Thousand Oaks, CA: Sage.
Stillman, J. (2010). *Narrative therapy trauma manual: A principle-based approach.* Minneapolis, MN: Caspersen.
White, M., & Epston, D. (1990). *Narrative means to therapeutic ends.* New York: Norton.
Winslade, J. M. (2009). Tracing lines of flight: Implications of the work of Giles Deleuze for narrative practice. *Family Process, 48*, 332–346.

# Poststructural Inquiry: Narrative Therapy's De-Centered and Influential Stance

**Stephen Gaddis**

**Abstract** This chapter unpacks narrative therapy's "de-centered and influential" stance. The de-centered and influential description is a response to the apparent ethical dilemma of not wanting to impose normative judgments in therapeutic conversations while simultaneously recognizing the impossibility of participating neutrally. Michael White, widely considered a founder of narrative therapy, highlights how certain practices of curiosity provide a way past this apparent philosophical dilemma. In this stance, narrative therapists take responsibility for their participation through the intentional use of questions that help deconstruct internalized stories and re-author alternative ones that clients identify as preferable. The author uses an extensive practice example to illustrate how de-centered and influential curiosity allows him to maintain his preferred narrative therapy stance.

## Background

I was introduced to narrative therapy (White 2007, 2011), and its poststructural foundations, in 1994 during my first MFT theory course at Colorado State University. I was drawn to it because of the way the approach centers poststructuralist perspectives on power and social justice (Combs and Freedman 2012; White and Epston 1990). Narrative therapy (Monk et al. 1997; Morgan 2000) has helped me know what I wish to strive for as a person and professional ever since. It has helped me understand the history of abuse I experienced as a child in ways that have been helpful, and it has helped me meet people in my work in ways they tell me has helped them. Though it has been my passion for over twenty years, I am still regularly challenged to live congruently with the ideas and ethics that are the center of narrative therapy.

While reflecting on understandings about power from a poststructural perspective, Michael White eventually came to describe the narrative therapist's stance as

S. Gaddis (✉)
Narrative Therapy Initiative, Salem, MA, USA
e-mail: srgaddis@mac.com



V. Dickerson (ed.), *Poststructural and Narrative Thinking in Family Therapy*,
AFTA SpringerBriefs in Family Therapy, DOI 10.1007/978-3-319-31490-7_2

"de-centered and influential" (White 1997, 2005). Many folks, including myself, have struggled to understand how it is possible to be *both* "de-centered" and "influential." It is this apparent contradiction that I address in this chapter. I illustrate my understandings about this ethical, political, and social-justice stance primarily through a detailed example from my work. Names and identifying information in this example have been changed to honor people's rights to privacy and anonymity. Before doing so, however, a brief review of key poststructural assumptions that underpin narrative therapy may be useful.

## Poststructuralism and Power

White drew his poststructural understanding about power primarily from Michael Foucault (Foucault 1980; Foucault et al. 1988, 2008; Rabinow 1991). Foucault, who was a French historian of ideas, helped extend understandings about power beyond popular and singular perspectives, if we understand power simply as the ability to influence. Popular notions of power in relationships typically have to do with concepts of domination and oppression, through practices of force and overt control (White 1997). The use of physical force, or its threat, is a power that shapes people's thoughts, feelings, and actions. If a woman is assaulted by a man, he can call on this form of power by saying, "If you tell anyone, I will kill you and your family." The threat of physical force to cause harm can powerfully influence the woman's potential response to the act of abuse.

Poststructural perspectives add a constitutionalist perspective to this popular power/force understanding (Dickerson 2014). Constitutionalist forms of power draw on *meaning-making* to influence people's behaviors, thoughts, and feelings. In the abuse example above, the man can call on this form of power by stating, "You are worthless, and no one but me would ever love you." The belief, or threat, that he might be "right" or represent "the truth" has the potential to influence the woman's experience of the abuse.

Popular understandings of power/force *repress* action through the threat of harm, while constitutionalist/poststructuralist understandings of power/knowledge *produce* "reality" through truth claims. Of course, both power/force and power/knowledge coexist today and are often tightly interwoven. Force is often used as a tactic to sustain privileged meanings, and privileged meanings are often used to justify the use of force.

## Internalizing Discourse and Normalizing Judgment

In poststructural theory, "discourse" is a word/concept used to identify and analyze domains of power/knowledge (Burr 2015; Hall 2001; Madigan and Law 1998; Polkinghorne 1988). Discourse describes those sets of meanings that have become culturally taken for granted about how things *should* be correctly understood. We know a discourse is present whenever forms of "should" are evoked or universal truth claims are expressed. Grounded in normalizing judgments, discourses do not typically feature concerns about diversity or context. Subjectivity is marginalized, and objectivity is privileged. Normalizing judgments often become internalized as objective truths, reflections of reality, or natural laws, and, therefore, frequently operate below people's awareness.

Perhaps a personal example can help illustrate discursive power and its operation through internalized normative judgment. When our son was in 5th grade, he decided to get his ear pierced. We were at the mall because his younger sister wanted to get pierced ears. She was caught by fear. Spontaneously, her brother told her that if it would help, he would get his ear pierced too to show her that it would be okay and not hurt too much. The next day after school, he came home in tears. His peers, boys and girls, teased him throughout the day. They derided him for being a girl and/or for being gay.

Clearly these young people had already internalized "truths" (i.e., culturally dominant discourses) that claim our son *should* understand he belongs in a category called "boys" and he *should* understand that wearing earrings is not what boys do, and he *should* understand it is bad for boys to be anything like girls and/or gay, which he *should* also understand are undesirable identities. These young people had already successfully internalized discursively generated, culturally venerated "norms" regarding gender and sexual identities. And, having been successfully internalized, those discourses were there to shape how these young people made sense of and responded to our son showing up at school with an earring.

The children in our son's class became agents of social control for the discursive truths linked to the patriarchal and heterosexist discourses that have emerged through contested histories of meaning-making. The children "policed" our son's act of wearing an earring, read by them as "abnormal," and acted to "correct" his failure to understand how he *should* know himself. Their tactics to bring things back to normal included acts of derision and teasing.

In the example with our son, at the local site of a predominantly white, liberal Montessori school classroom in a financially and educationally privileged community, the dominance of patriarchal and heterosexist discourses influenced how things were being measured and understood. What's so insidious is that these children, and likely their parents, if asked, would probably say they do not support patriarchy or heterosexism, and yet, those normative truth regimes were powerfully influencing what was actually taking place.

Sadly, the policing of our son worked. He decided to take the earring out the next day. He told his friends that I had made him get it. Even more sadly, the story about him being a person who cared about helping his younger sister was stolen by these gender and heterosexist truth claims. Though my wife and I did our best to help him understand the problem from this perspective, we were not going to force him to wear an earring to protest normative judgements and endure more abuse. His prize, for taking out the earring, was being welcomed back to "normal," its modicum of "moral worth," and the associated absence of derision and other forms of abuse!

## Helping Professions and Power/Knowledge

Discursive power has the potential to operate wherever relationships take place, including between therapists and clients. A narrative therapy approach helps conceptualize problems in terms of the *relationship* between people and stories, not in terms of individual pathologies, irrational cognitions, or dysfunctional family systems (Bird 2000; White 1995). Problems, from a narrative perspective, are understood as internalized stories that have negative effects on the life of the person and/or the people in their lives. Internalized stories are invariably supported by culturally dominant discourses.

Narrative therapists are interested in helping to create a separation between people and internalized stories so people can explore the effects of their relationships with these stories on various domains of their lives (Bird 2008; White 2007; White and Epston 1990). From this position, "clients" can critique and revise their relationships with stories according to their preferences. In doing so, it becomes possible for them to develop alternative relationships with stories they identify as preferable.

Since all relational activities involve storying, therapists cannot take a position of neutrality in their contributions to these alternative stories. We are at risk of acting as agents of social control for discursive truths linked to professional perspectives. We are implicated in whatever preferred stories may be emerging in helping contexts. This raises the question of how therapists are going to both acknowledge the impossibility of neutrality while simultaneously holding a preference for not "imposing" stories on clients' lives, including normative professional ones.

With this question in front of us, we can begin to unpack the de-centered and influential stance White described (Morgan 2006; White 1997, 2005). The "de-centered" dimension has to do with an awareness of whose knowledges are privileged in any conversation. In a therapeutic context, clients' lives are the subject; thus, clients' knowledges take priority over therapists' knowledges. Clients are positioned as primary authors when it comes to loading meaning onto events in their lives.

The "influential" dimension has to do with the therapist's response to the meanings that clients are offering. In narrative therapy, "influence" involves responses that help create a relational space between clients and stories, and that help clients develop alternative stories that feature their values, hopes, intentions, purposes, and commitments (White 2007).

One of White's most significant contributions was showing how curiosity in therapeutic contexts allows us to be radically respectful and non-judgmental while meticulously opening new possibilities for people to live through alternative stories. These skills of curiosity take place in two broad domains of narrative practice: deconstructing and re-authoring.

Curiosity skills in deconstructing feature questions that have to do with carefully unpacking the real effects of the internalized stories on clients' lives and relationships, and re-contextualizing the internalized stories back into the histories of their subjective constructions. For re-authoring, questions allow clients to link events in their lives with intentional state understandings that help form a counterplot for people to shape their lives and relationships in preferred ways. In both cases, skills of scaffolding are critical.

Scaffolding is the ability to adjust questions so that clients are able to answer from their domains of knowledge and imagination. Scaffolding skills involve listening to a client's expression and forming questions that are linked to the particular expression in the service of either deconstruction or re-authoring. And, if a person is unable to answer a question, scaffolding involves therapists adjusting questions so it becomes more possible for clients to answer.

Deconstructing and re-authoring practices are both in the service of rich story development, which is the expressed purpose of narrative therapy. White (2007) offers various maps of practice for achieving rich story development. These maps of practice include externalizing conversations, re-authoring conversations, and re-membering conversations, among others. All of these conversational maps implicitly include a de-centered and influential position because privileging clients' knowledges and accepting the impossibility of conversational neutrality is a foundational ethic in narrative therapy.

I like to imagine what a world might look like if we took turns being de-centered and influential with one another, rather than policing each other according to cultural norms. In this imagined world, I like to think our son would have his earring met by his peers with questions about what wearing it meant to him and how it was connected to what he valued.

## A Practice Example

About nine months ago, I received a call from Linda wondering if I could help her 13-year-old son, Ben. We didn't have much time to talk, and I said I didn't know if I would be able to help but that I would be happy to try. I asked if she wanted to meet to discuss her concerns more thoroughly. She thought that might be a good thing to do, and I asked who she thought might make sense to attend this initial meeting. She thought it best to start with herself and her partner, David. She and David lived together with Ben and his older brother, Tim, and two older sisters, Jen and Wren.

## Meeting 1

At our first meeting, Linda and David described Ben as a person who is "competitive and combative"; "socially way behind"; "disrespectful"; "not someone who follows through with things"; "very immature"; and "insistent that his way is the right way."

I noticed Ben was being characterized according to pathological narratives, and problems were being located in Ben's "self." I was not surprised these ways of understanding were what was most available to them. In Western culture, undesirable actions and feelings are most easily storied as evidence of a disordered self (i.e., irrational thinking, mental illness, and trauma). I don't support these internalized ways of understanding. Equally important to me is not locating the problem in Linda or in the family.

So, I inquired with Linda about how her wish to tell me about these problems was linked to what is important to her. She explained she was worried about the quality of Ben's life if he continued on his current path. She explained that she didn't think he was able to face difficult feelings and shared, "He hides away anytime he feels angry, sad, or upset. He crawls into cabinets and stays inside them for a very long time."

I inquired about some of the significant events in the history of Ben's life. Linda explained that she and Ben's father, Brad, ended their relationship about ten years previously. Brad now lives in another country, and Ben in past years moved back and forth between his mom and dad. Currently, there is no intention for Ben to return to live with Brad in the future. In this conversation with Linda and David, whenever Brad was spoken about by Linda, there were vague references to him being "different."

At the end of the first meeting, it was decided that Linda and Ben would attend the second meeting together, without David, since Linda and Ben seemed to have a close relationship and Linda thought that might help Ben feel a bit more comfortable. After this meeting, it was clear to me that Ben was facing differing crises at home, in school, and especially around his identity.

## Meeting 2

I try to take time to orient my thinking before meetings. In this case, while reviewing my notes from the meeting with Linda and David, I was clear that I did not want to make sense of Ben's behaviors as manifestations of some developmental or mental disorder. Rather, I considered his actions as performances of stories he had internalized. I assumed these internalized stories were ones that he had been recruited into and not ones radically made up by him alone. I assumed it was unlikely he had a history of being invited into a position where he was the primary author of his life. I assumed whatever stories he had internalized did not necessarily reflect his preferences.

I also wanted to be respectful of Linda's concerns about the problems she witnessed and experienced, and especially her care for Ben's life. So, when Ben arrived with his mom at the next meeting, I asked whether he shared his mother's care and concern about his life and his life's path. He said he did indeed still care and was pretty uncertain why things were the way they were currently.

I shared that I had learned from his mom that he had lived in different countries and with different family members. I asked him permission to learn more about some of the history of his life up to this point. I wondered what it had been like for him to be such an experienced international traveler at such a young age. I wondered whether that had been easy or hard, or not something he had thought about.

He shared that living with "different rules" had been pretty hard. I learned that he had to endure and respond to some significant bullying in his previous school when he was living with his father. He explained that he had gotten into some trouble and was sent to a "bad kid" school, which also had been hard. I asked what happened that got him sent to a "bad kid" school. He said a teacher was looking at his sister in a "creepy" way so he pushed the teacher to make him stop. The teacher was so outraged he insisted Ben be expelled from school. At the end of our initial meeting, Ben asked if he could come alone for our next meeting. I agreed, assuming there was some important intention on his part for this request, though I didn't know what it might be.

## Meeting 3

*My intention in preparing for this meeting was to (1) maintain a de-centered and influential stance, (2) help deconstruct totalizing problem-saturated identity stories, and (3) help re-author some alternative story that Ben would prefer and that would enhance his sense of "personal agency."*

**Ben** I was on the bus yesterday thinking about something I want to talk with you about.

**Steve** Wow! I don't usually experience people thinking in advance like that before meeting with me. What were you thinking we could talk about?

**Ben** I wanted to ask you what I should do about my anger.
(Long Pause)

**Steve** You know, sometimes people think that because I am a therapist I have lots of answers to those kinds of questions. But after meeting with many people, I have learned that each person's relationship with anger is a little different. Would it be okay with you if I take some time to get to know what kind of anger we are talking about here that is creating problems for you? Would it be okay for me to ask some questions instead of me having an answer to your question?

**Ben** Sure.

**Steve** Can you tell me anything about this anger that might help me start to understand it better?

*I am intentionally de-centering myself by not taking up the invitation to be an expert on anger, while also acting influentially by locating "anger" in a relational space in my question.*

**Ben** It builds up inside me.

**Steve** Okay, it builds up inside you. How long would you say it has been building up? Has that been happening for a long time or is this something kind of new, or …?

**Ben** It's been building up in me for a long time.

**Steve** So, this anger has been around for a long time. Do you know how or when this anger may have entered your life?

**Ben** Well, when I was seven my cousin told on me when I took a cookie from a cookie jar, and I was so angry I started choking him.

**Steve** Okay, when you were seven, this anger got you to choke your cousin. This is helping me know more about this anger. Was there something about what happened with your cousin that bothered you or was this okay with you?

**Ben** I didn't like hurting him.

**Steve** Were you surprised the anger got you to hurt him or was it something you planned or expected to happen?

**Ben** No. It just jumped out.

**Steve** So, this anger jumped out and got you to hurt your cousin when you were seven, and it surprised you. And you didn't like that this anger got you to hurt someone. Would you say this anger has been trying to find ways to jump out of you since that time, or is it something that kind of goes away and makes comebacks?

**Ben** It is there a lot but I try to keep it inside rather than let it jump out and hurt people, but it keeps building up inside me.

*Stories (and relationships) have histories that take place over time. Thus, my questions are tracing the history of the development of this relationship while helping Ben characterize anger further. To further deconstruct this story/relationship, it will be helpful to hear about more times the anger had influence.*

**Steve** Can you tell me about a time recently when you felt this anger building inside you again?

**Ben** Yea, in school today. My teacher was trying to explain something, and I didn't understand what she was saying.

**Steve** You felt anger building when you didn't understand the teacher?

**Ben** Yea.

**Steve** Do you have any guesses about how not understanding the teacher might have helped the anger grow?

**Ben** I'm not sure.

**Steve** Were you hoping to understand the material in class?

**Ben** Yea.

**Steve** Okay, so you were caring about understanding the material. Did you think about what you might need to do to get the understanding and learning you wanted?

**Ben** Umm… I would have to admit I didn't understand and ask for help.

**Steve** Are not understanding and asking for help things that would be okay or not okay?

**Ben** Not okay.

**Steve** So, do you think anger grew from ideas that it is not okay to not know things and need help?

**Ben** Yea.

**Steve** What is not okay about not knowing something or having to ask for help?

**Ben** It means I am weak.

**Steve** What is not okay about feeling weak?

**Ben** It makes me feel sad and sorry for myself.

*I have worked to stay de-centered and not load meanings for him. I am not interpreting or suggesting how he might understand anything. I also am asking questions that are influential in the sense they are about what ideas "anger" needs to have power. In other words, my questions are making discourse visible. I am not surprised by the ideas named and exposed, given the dominance of patriarchal and individualist discourses in Western culture. What I don't know yet is the particular history of how Ben was recruited into such a strong relationship with these ideas and ways of understanding.*

**Steve** Okay, so the anger grew from ideas about it not being okay to not know something and needing to ask for help to learn, and ideas of being weak and sad or sorry for yourself. Were you able to keep the anger from jumping out in the classroom when these ideas and feelings were helping build anger?

**Ben** Yea.

**Steve** If it had jumped out, would it have gotten you to hurt the teacher, or you, or both, or neither?

**Ben** Both. It would have me wanting to hurt her for not teaching me well and me for not understanding.

**Steve** Okay, so how did you keep it from jumping out?

**Ben** I just kept it in me, but it is really hard. I didn't have any place to go hide, which is what I mostly do when the anger builds up inside me.

**Steve** There are many more questions I would like to ask to learn about how you figured out how to hide to keep the anger from getting you to hurt people, but I find myself wondering where you got the idea that not knowing something and asking for help is not okay, and that feeling weak and sad and sorry for yourself is not okay?

**Ben** When I lived with my dad he wanted to train me to be an … I guess you could say, "alpha male."

**Steve** What do you mean?

*Ben then told me stories about how his father put him in situations to "toughen him up." For example, he dropped him in a forest at 6 years old and told him to find his way home. He took him camping and had him prove his strength by making him take something out of a campfire with his bare hands without showing pain.*

*Through further inquiry, Ben named and described the various ways of being that are valued in an "alpha male" world. These include a pyramidal structure with one "dominant man" who controls resources, relates through acts of intimidation, does not show feelings other than rage, and engages in random acts of power that remind everyone else they are not the most physically strong person. When I asked about women and girls, he concluded they have such a low ranking in an alpha male world that they are not considered real threats. He spontaneously volunteered that may be why his mom left his dad.*

*I asked what he thought about these ways of being and whether they were ones he liked or not. He shared that he would intentionally make his dad mad at times as a way to not accept the total submission the alpha male world expected from someone "weaker." Throughout his sharing, tears were present for him.*

*I was concerned that he just revealed that he was violating lots of alpha male expectations by telling me these stories and showing tears, for example. How would he know whether I am a man who stands for or against alpha male ways of being? I didn't think it would be neutral for me to say nothing. I didn't want to leave his understanding to chance; however, I also was concerned about putting myself at the center of meaning-making.*

**Steve** Would it be helpful to know what I think about the alpha male world, or would you rather not know?

**Ben** It would be good to know.

**Steve** I believe I have spent my whole life trying to find places to live that are outside the alpha male world because I was really hurt by the alpha male world as a boy. I am strongly against the alpha male world. Part of the reason I became a therapist is because I want to build a different world than the alpha male one. Can I ask how it is for you to learn that I stand against the alpha male world?

**Ben** It's a huge relief.

**Steve** Do you know why it might be such a big relief?

**Ben** I don't feel alone and I was afraid to say how I really felt.

*For him to be able to take a position against the alpha male world, he must have at least some knowledge about some other possibility. Every knowing is a discernment and no single story can account for all lived experiences. Whatever subjugated knowledges he has, however, I believe are not well developed. He must have subjugated stories about different possible ways of being that he might prefer.*

**Steve** So if you had a say for yourself, would your preference be to stand for an alpha male world or some other world?

**Ben** Some other world.

**Steve** Have you seen or experienced anything other than the alpha male world during your life? Like in books or families, or animals, or movies, or …

**Ben** Yea. I have seen them on TV and in movies but they aren't real.

**Steve** If there was a real world that was outside the alpha male world, would that be something you would want?

**Ben** It'd be great.

**Steve** What name might you give these other worlds that you've seen on TV or in the movies that may or may not be real?

**Ben** I don't know, …maybe… I guess… a "moral world."

*Alternative stories start with words and descriptions that through inquiry become much more richly developed.*

**Steve** Okay, a moral world. (Pause) Can you describe how a moral world might be different from an alpha male one?

**Ben** No.

**Steve** Would it be okay for me to ask some questions about what might be in this moral world if you got to have a say about it?

**Ben** Sure.

**Steve** In the alpha male world, if I understand right, ideas about not knowing and needing help are not okay. Would you want them to be okay or not okay in the moral world?

**Ben** They would be okay.

**Steve** What about feelings like sadness, would they be okay or not okay in the moral world?

**Ben** It would be okay to show emotions.

**Steve** So, I just want to see if I understand correctly, the tears that were present when you were telling me about the stories with your dad that caused you pain would be okay in the moral world?

**Ben** Yes.

**Steve** I also was learning that in the alpha male world, only one man gets to be most important, and that other men are always threats that need to be kept in place, and that women and girls are not equal to either men or boys. In the moral world, would this be how things were ordered, or would you prefer something else.

**Ben** Everyone would be equal.

*Newly developed stories require careful capturing for people to be able to keep extending and reflecting on them. I am thinking we have covered a lot of territory and it might be a good time to summarize our conversation. This allows him a reflecting surface to develop his thinking further.*

**Steve** Okay, in the moral world everyone would be equal, and it would be okay for people to have feelings like sadness, and for people to not always know things, and sometimes feel weak. I'm just wondering how people would be relating to each other when there were problems in this moral world that you are describing, which I'm finding myself more and more interested in. In the alpha male world, things are worked out through actions that include intimidation and physical strength. Would these be as important in a moral world, or would there be other ways people would work things out together?

**Ben** I guess there would be talking and listening, and negotiating. My brother doesn't care that smoking pot affects me. I don't want to bring my friends over ever because the house always smells like pot and I would be embarrassed. My brother doesn't care. My mom doesn't listen when I tell her this is a problem for me.

*I want to maintain my preference for separating problems and people, and I don't want to locate the problem in Linda or his brother. Instead, I think that the problem has to do with different stories that foster different ways of being and skills for relating.*

**Steve** In this moral world we are imagining together, would your brother and mother be responding differently than they have been?

**Ben** Yes. They would listen and care.

**Steve** We learned about the principles that are most important in the alpha male world, would listening and caring be important in a moral world?

**Ben** Yes. And fairness would be important too.

**Steve** Okay, that is helpful for me to know. Fairness is a principle that would be important in a moral world. If listening and care were offered to you as responses to how your brother's smoking pot is affecting your life and relationships with your friends, what effects do you think it might have?

**Ben** I don't know.

**Steve** Do you think it might create some feelings or thoughts?

**Ben** Some feelings, I think.

**Steve** So maybe some feelings. Can you imagine what one feeling might be that listening and caring might create for you?

**Ben** It's hard.

**Steve** It's hard to know what the feeling might be?

**Ben** Yea.

**Steve** What name might be a good one for the feeling that is hard to imagine?

**Ben** Sentimental, I guess.

**Steve** Okay, can we use sentimental for the time being? Would this sentimental feeling be a good thing, not so good, or something else?

**Ben** It would be a good thing because it is not hard for me to say good-bye to people or let go of people. If someone were saying good-bye to me and I knew I wouldn't see them ever again, I would just say, "bye," not, "I love you." Like, when my grandfather died. The next day was just another day. I didn't have any feelings.

**Steve** Would you say that not having feelings could have been an outcome of alpha male trainings, or something else?

**Ben** I hadn't thought about that, but yea, alpha male training. Maybe it's an instinct now from being brainwashed.

**Steve** How much training would you say you have had for growing sentimental feelings?

**Ben** Zero.

**Steve** If you had more training for sentimental feelings and more of a chance to live in a moral world, do you think that could be helpful in some way?

**Ben** Yea. I could have more of a conscience. I really don't know my identity.

**Steve** Could caring about having a conscience be part of your identity?

**Ben** Yea.

**Steve** Would standing for a moral world, fairness, caring, and listening be something that could be part of your identity, or would that not be something you would want?

**Ben** I like that!

**Steve** Would supporting emotions like sentimentality and standing against ideas that claim weakness is bad and not knowing something is bad also be part of how you might like to become what you stand for as a person?

**Ben** Yea!

**Steve** I've been learning so much and I have so many more questions, but I am wondering if the next time we meet we could explore whether what we have been learning might give us some possible answers to your question about what to do with the anger that builds up in you and might want to jump out and have you hurt people, or that gets you to have to hide to keep from hurting people?

**Ben** For sure!

**Steve** How has this meeting been for you?

**Ben** It's been really nice. I don't have people to talk with about these things that I think.

*Two juxtaposed stories are now beginning to come alongside one another, allowing Ben to potentially experience more choices for thinking, feeling, and acting. The dominant alpha male story is being a bit troubled by the emerging moral world one.*

## Meeting 4

**Steve** Has it been more of an alpha male world or moral world since we last met?

**Ben** My brother's girlfriend threw my laundry from the washing machine on the floor because she wanted to clean her clothes. I tried talking nicely to my brother and asked him to tell her not to do that again.

**Steve** How did it go?

**Ben** He didn't care.

**Steve** Did anger jump out or did you hide or did you find a third way?

**Ben** I started yelling.

**Steve** Was that from anger building up?

**Ben** Yea.

**Steve** What do you think the anger might be connected to that was important to you?

**Ben** A better chance of being heard.

**Steve** So you were caring about being heard. What is it like to not have him care or listen?

**Ben** It's degrading.

**Steve** Okay, degrading. If your chances of being heard and cared about are low by people who are stuck in an alpha male world, do you have some other ideas about how you might respond to degrading acts?

**Ben** No. If I calmly say, "I don't appreciate how you are talking to me," I won't get heard and when I try to tell my mom, she says, "Don't let it bother you."

**Steve** Do you find the suggestion to not let it bother you helpful?

**Ben** No.

**Steve** How come you wanted to tell your mom?

**Ben** I'm hoping she might tell him it isn't okay for his girlfriend to do things like that and to basically get him to stop doing things that bother me. But, when she talks to him he just blows her off. I think she has given up on him.

**Steve** Do you think there might be any other things she could do that might help, other than telling him to stop, when she hears that you are experiencing a problem with how you are being treated?

**Ben** I don't know.

*I am starting to think and learn about some of the real predicaments and challenges that Ben is up against in linking his preferences for a moral world. I think Ben has a right to have these challenges acknowledged and responded to in some way.*

**Steve** Does anyone else come to mind who might have ideas about how to respond when you feel degraded?

**Ben** Not my dad or David. I want to leave and be on my own but I don't have the money or independence. I have to just wait.

**Steve** Do you think it might be helpful if we invited your mother to come to a meeting to try to help her understand the kind of challenge you feel like you are facing, and to explore how she might listen in ways that might be different and more helpful, and see if she was interested in joining this project of building a moral world?

**Ben** Well… I think if we open her eyes too much it could really hurt her, and she has been through a lot already with my dad. And, I'm not sure if she can.

**Steve** Okay. What do you think it might say about you that despite how much hurt you are experiencing you don't want to do something to hurt your mom, even if it might help you?

**Ben** I'm not sure.

**Steve** Would it be okay to share that the word that comes to my mind is "kind"?

**Ben** Yes. Kind. I really do think I am kind but it comes and goes a lot.

*At this point, I have a sense that for the moral world story to have a chance to become more "real," it is necessary for it to be linked to some community that might authenticate and legitimize his hopes and intentions, and share knowledges they may have about how they have navigated the challenges they have faced in standing for a moral world* (Gaddis et al. 2014).

**Steve** I'd like to come back to hear some stories about you knowing you are kind, but before that I am still struck by this real problem that you are up against. I am not sure how you can best respond to being treated in degrading ways if the person who is treating you that way is not interested in caring. I'm not sure what you can do if you are not okay with being treated in degrading ways and can't find a way to make it stop or find someone who can help you make it stop. I have this weird idea. I am teaching a course to a lot of people this weekend who are thinking about how they might help people who are experiencing problems like the one you are facing. Would it be all right for me to ask them if they have any stories from their own lives about how they might have responded to a problem like the one you are facing?

**Ben** Sure!

**Steve** Great. I will collect any stories they have to share and we can look at them together to see if there are ideas that you might find helpful and supports your interest in living in a moral world.

**Ben** Cool.

*I did not want to leave him without any response to this dilemma. There were many options I could have chosen but in this moment I decide to briefly center myself. I share a story from my life in a way that locates it in my subjective experience and then re-position him to see if he can relate and, if so, why, which would return him to the center of the conversation.*

**Steve** You have me thinking about times I think a similar problem was messing with me. Would it be all right to share it with you?

**Ben** Sure.

**Steve** Could we agree that these are things that helped me and they may be different from things that could help you?

**Ben** Sure.

**Steve** Well, I hadn't thought too much about this before our conversation, but as I think back, I guess I felt pretty trapped when I was your age. I didn't like the alpha male world and did not feel like anyone really knew how to help me, including me. I think I listened to a lot of music and when I think back on the music I liked, it had a lot to do with keeping me close to the kind of world I wanted in the future for myself. Even more importantly, I think, I decided I wanted to have a family of my own some day and I didn't want to pass any of the things that hurt me onto my own children. I think that dream really helped me keep connected to what I wanted for my life. I don't think anyone saw it, however, which made it harder for me to keep it in my own awareness.

**Ben** Hmmm.

**Steve** I'm really happy you've helped me think about this right now because when I think back on my 13-year-old self, I would want to tell him that was a smart way to stay close to his hopes and that eventually it worked out really well. What is it like for you to hear me tell you this story from my life?

**Ben** Really good.

**Steve** Why?

**Ben** I don't feel so alone, and it gives me something I can think about for myself.

I followed through and gathered many letters from the students in my class about his hopes and predicaments. He found these letters quite moving. Following his positive reaction, I wondered if he might be interested in having a meeting with another person who I meet with in my work. I explained to Ben that Bobby was someone who had come to see me because he was unhappy about how Anger was getting him to treat members of his family. I told him that Bobby's life had been significantly negatively affected by the alpha male world and that he was someone who has worked hard to re-claim his life from the brainwashing he received. I concluded that I knew Bobby highly valued caring and kindness, especially if it meant contributing to the well being of young people.

Ben was very interested, so after getting permission from his mother, this meeting took place. It was full of tears and sharing stories. After the meeting, Bobby wrote a letter that Ben found highly meaningful. Ben reported to me that he was surprised that someone would continue to think about him and take the time to do something for him in that way.

After getting Bobby's letter, Ben thought he would like to invite David into a meeting to catch him up on his intentions to live in a moral world. David agreed and we had a powerfully moving time together where David expressed a complete interest in joining in on this moral world project.

Throughout these meetings, I was doing some co-research with Ben (Epston 1999; Gaddis 2004). We were studying whether the development of his interest in a moral world was having any real effects in his life.

Ben told me stories about choosing different kinds of friends based on his evaluation of their position in either an alpha male or moral world. For instance, he told a story about a friend who was very "accepting and calm" and "not trying to control things," and how he downgraded a friend who "always insists I do what he wants to do" and thinks it's "fun to knee me in the stomach whenever he wants." He distinguished people who are interested in "just taking" from people who are interested in "give and take."

He said he noticed more feelings of sentimentality and that led him to want to re-connect with a friend from his past who he'd lost contact with. He told me a powerfully moving story of a friend who confided in him that she was feeling suicidal. He said he chose to let himself feel sadness because he thought showing those feelings to her might help her not feel alone and that he wanted to be there for her. He said she seemed shocked that someone would want to go out of their way to care for her.

He reported that he didn't experience anger building up in him anymore. He explained he now had a different anger but it didn't leave him feeling like he would hurt anyone, including himself. When I asked what he thought he may have done to get rid of the alpha male anger and replace it with a moral world anger, he shared that he just kept thinking about "the meetings" that we've had and the letters that he's received. He also said he was developing a practice of distracting himself when alpha males tried to bother him.

He told one story about how there was an alpha male peer taunting him and he decided to distract himself by going for a bike ride instead. He said there was a lot of "proof" he was really "transitioning" from an alpha male world to a moral world, and that he guessed he was about 25 % of the way there. He shared that he wasn't having to hide in cabinets anymore. He reported that David was doing things differently, now "going out of his way to notice me and show care." He volunteered, "I feel like I can be more of 'kid' now," which produced some tears of happiness from me.

I also was asking Linda to let me know if there were any changes in her concerns about Ben's path. Linda sent me an e-mail reply to my question about whether her worry for Ben was as strong as when we met. She wrote, "I see a very positive change in Ben. That alpha male stuff is hardly around anymore." I found this very interesting since she and I had never talked about the alpha male stuff.

In our most recent meeting, I asked Ben if I could review the changes that have happened since we met. I believe it is critical to keep telling and re-telling the developing preferred story, since my experience is that the old dominant story will not relinquish its relationship with Ben easily. I prepared a two-page report on all that I had learned from our meetings that seemed important, and when I was finished sharing all the steps he had taken to transition from an alpha male world to a moral one, he stated, "I have a completely different mindset than I did when we first met." Based on this comment and my wish to continue extending his story into still larger communities of support, I asked Ben if I could share another idea with him.

I explained I was doing some teaching the next week at a two-day workshop. I thought it might be helpful to my teaching if I could share our work and thought people attending might be interested in knowing about and potentially joining Ben's moral world project. I said one way we could do this was to meet again and videotape a review of our work. I said I also would like to ask him to help me understand more about this "completely different mindset" that he mentioned.

We arranged for his mom to drive him to my office on a Sunday, and I videotaped our meeting. I played the entire 40-minute video at the workshop and asked people to write outsider witness responses to what they watched. I collected 30 letters from workshop participants that we read together at our next meeting. Ben reflected on each letter after it was read. Then, after we finished reading them all, I asked what the effects of these letters were for him.

**Ben** "At first it was kind of like, I guess in the beginning it was mostly like ideas. Now it is turning into sort of an ideology."

**Steve** What is the difference between ideas and ideologies?

**Ben** Ideas, people sort of listen to them, but ideologies are something people try to stay with and try to like almost have responsibility to stay with.

**Steve** Would you say that is a good thing or a bad thing, or …?

**Ben** I'd say it is a good thing. There are people who really do believe change is needed, and it is spreading. I feel like after that teaching, they probably went home and their work place and were talking about it with their friends and stuff.

**Steve** What's it like thinking you may have contributed to people either remembering or deciding or being inspired to an ideology and commitment?

**Ben** It is almost like, really crazy, to wrap my head around, because you are always supposed to find your own type of role model, and I'm not trying to be cocky or anything, but it almost feels like I am being other people's role model.

**Steve** What it is like to think you may be representing a role model for people?

**Ben** It is mind-blowing (laughs).

**Steve** Do you like it?

**Ben** Yea, it is something I can get even more behind, since I am already behind it.

We put each letter into a clear sheet that now live collectively in a three-ring binder, which he named, "The Moral Pack." He intends to draw a wolf as a symbol of the pack. He identified the motto for the pack, which is to "Strive, Thrive, and Advance." As you might imagine, these meetings with Ben have been significantly meaningful to me personally and professionally. This two-way contribution helps sustain me in doing this hard work.

I am grateful for the ways people I meet in my work inspire me and keep me connected to hope for myself and the world. For the past two decades, I have been striving to think and live in ways that are congruent with a Narrative Worldview and its relational ethics and stance. White's description of a de-centered and influential stance, and its link to poststructural understandings of power, has offered me a language for ways of being that help me move closer to my preferred "self" in all domains of my life.

## References


Bird, J. (2000). *The heart's narrative: Therapy and navigating life's contradictions*. Auckland, NZ: Edge Press.

Bird, J. (2008). *Constructing narratives to make a difference*. Auckland, NZ: Edge Press.

Burr, V. (2015). *Social constructionism*. London: Routledge.

Combs, G., & Freedman, J. (2012). Narrative, poststructuralism, and social justice. Current practices in narrative therapy. *The Counseling Psychologist, 40*(7), 1033–1060.

Dickerson, V. C. (2014). The advance of poststructuralism and its influence on family therapy. *Family Process, 53*(3), 401–414.

Epston, D. (1999). *Co-research: The making of an alternative knowledge: Narrative therapy and community work: A conference collection*. Adelaide: Dulwich Centre Publications.

Foucault, M. (1980). *Power/knowledge: Selected interviews and other writings, 1972–1977*. New York: Pantheon.
Foucault, M., Lagrange, J., Burchell, G., & Davidson, A. I. (2008). *Psychiatric power: Lectures at the college de france, 1973–1974*. New York: Picador.
Foucault, M., Martin, L. H., Gutman, H., & Hutton, P. H. (1988). *Technologies of the self: A seminar with Michel Foucault*. Amherst, MA: University of Massachusetts Press.
Gaddis, S. (2004). Re-positioning traditional research: Centring clients' accounts in the construction of professional therapy knowledges. *International Journal of Narrative Therapy & Community Work, 2004*(2), 1.
Gaddis, S. R., Kotzé, E., & Hulme, T. (2014). Peach trees grow in the spaces between people: Counselling practices in the territory of violence. *Australian and New Zealand Journal of Family Therapy, 35*(3), 353–363.
Hall, S. (2001). Foucault: Power, knowledge and discourse. *Discourse Theory and Practice: A Reader, 72*, 81.
Madigan, S., & Law, I. (1998). *Praxis: Situating discourse, feminism and politics in narrative therapies*. Vancouver: Yaletown Family Therapy.
Monk, G., Winslade, J., Crocket, K., & Epston, D. (1997). *Narrative therapy in practice: The archaeology of hope*. San Francisco: Jossey-Bass Publishers.
Morgan, A. (2000). *What is narrative therapy. An easy-to-read introduction*. Adelaide, South Australia: Dulwich Centre Publications.
Morgan, A. (2006). The position of the therapist in working with children and their families. In M. White & A. Morgan (Eds.), *Narrative therapy with children and their families*. Adelaide, South Australia: Dulwich Centre Publications.
Polkinghorne, D. E. (1988). *Narrative knowing and the human sciences*. Albany, NY: SUNY Press.
Rabinow, P. (1991). *The Foucault reader*. London: Penguin.
White, M. (1995). *The narrative perspective in therapy: Reauthoring lives, interviews and essays*. Adelaide, South Australia: Dulwich Centre Publications.
White, M. (1997). *Narratives of therapists' lives*. Adelaide, South Australia: Dulwich Centre Publications.
White, M. (2005). *Workshop notes*. Retrieved from www.dulwichcentre.com.au
White, M. (2007). *Maps of narrative practice*. New York: WW Norton & Company.
White, M. (2011). *Narrative practice: Continuing the conversations*. New York: WW Norton & Company.
White, M., & Epston, D. (1990). *Narrative means to therapeutic ends*. New York: WW Norton & Company.

# Re-imagining Family: Growing Family Therapy Practice from the Rhizome of Autoethnography

**Elmarie Kotzé, Andrew Kulasingham and Kathie Crocket**

**Abstract** This chapter explores a therapist's autoethnography and the subsequent shaping effects of his self-in-relation, for him and his therapy practice. The autoethnography employed narrative therapy's re-membering practices to (re)write into existence an enriched relationship with the therapist's deceased mother. This process produced movements through which he and his family were transformed. In Deleuzo-Guattarian terms, *becoming different* became possible in surprising and delightful ways that he did not foresee when he began his autoethnography. The final section of the chapter turns to how these new *becomings* played out rhizomatically in the therapist's family therapy.

## Introduction

Family therapy has long concerned itself with the significance of the therapist's self-in-relation. Extending this tradition, narrative therapy pays attention to the narratives of therapists' own lives (White 1997), that is the ways in which we as therapists draw on our own storied life experiences in our therapy practices. Furthermore, White's (2007) exposition of a two-way account of therapy suggests that every therapeutic encounter also shapes the therapist's life. This chapter extends these emphases of narrative therapy by drawing on an aspect of the autoethnographic research of one therapist, Andrew, and its reappearance in his family therapy practice in a way that we describe as rhizomatic. Andrew, Elmarie, and Kathie write this chapter together out of the different learning opportunities of

E. Kotzé (✉) · K. Crocket
University of Waikato, Hamilton, New Zealand
e-mail: elmariek@waikato.ac.nz

K. Crocket
e-mail: kcrocket@waikato.ac.nz

A. Kulasingham
ImpacTauranga, Tauranga, New Zealand
e-mail: kula.andrew@gmail.com



V. Dickerson (ed.), *Poststructural and Narrative Thinking in Family Therapy*,
AFTA SpringerBriefs in Family Therapy, DOI 10.1007/978-3-319-31490-7_3

this autoethnography for each of us: Andrew as researcher and family therapist, Elmarie as teacher and research supervisor, and Kathie as teacher and therapy supervisor.

Narrative therapy emerged from the linguistic and discursive turns in philosophy (White and Epston 1990) exemplified by the work of poststructuralist philosophers such as Foucault and Derrida. Narrative therapy's central explanatory metaphor was and continues to be the story, but always a story situated in the socio-cultural–political realm. In emphasising that identity is a social achievement, White (1997) developed a range of practices that recruit audiences to the stories people tell about their lives (outsider witnessing, see White 2007), or that select others into association with a person's life (re-membering practices, see White 2007). This chapter builds from these familiar metaphors and practices of narrative therapy, by entering some new territories that narrative therapy has begun to explore. In regard to such ongoing explorations, Winslade (2009) described Michael White as "always searching for new ways to describe this work [therapy], combing the writings of creative thinkers for inspiration" (p. 345). This chapter makes a small contribution to that quest, in a number of steps.

We first suggest that developments in autoethnographic research provide the therapy field with concepts and methods to investigate the territory of the therapist's self-in-relation. Such explorations provide a possibility for what Dickerson (2014, p. 412) advocates for twenty-first-century family therapy—"a more complex understanding of context, of multiplicity and of social justice". We introduce autoethnography as a research genre where, in the process of writing, self and culture are brought into dialogue, asserting multiplicity. We then show how Andrew employed narrative therapy's remembering practices in an autoethnographic exploration of his relationship with his deceased mother, Ranji. At the same time, we take a turn to the explanatory metaphor of the rhizome (Deleuze and Guattari 1987). This is a step that fits with the traditions of narrative therapy as it continues to value curiosity in the to and fro of therapy and in theorising practice (White 1991). The turn is also a rhizomatic growth from the work of both White and Winslade (see Winslade 2009) who more recently applied the work of Deleuze in analysing therapeutic conversation.

Deleuze and Guattari (1987) argue that traditional thought tends to follow the familiar linear and hierarchical pattern of a tree—it has roots, a trunk, and branches. By contrast, a rhizome, a rootstock which often grows in unexpected directions, "has no middle: no trunk. It has no end: no leaves. It is always in the middle, always in process" (May 2005, p. 133). A rhizome connects and opens space in-between, it subverts hierarchy, and it cannot be reduced to a single point or radical core (Conley 2006). The metaphor of a rhizome, we suggest, offers an opportunity to extend thinking about therapy, and about the therapist's self-in-relation, beyond ideas about linearity, cause and effect. The rhizome appears at various points in this chapter, offering us possibilities to show self-as-process, a self-in-relation in the midst of movement: in Deleuze and Guattari's terms also a "becoming", as we show shortly.

## Autoethnographic Writing

Autoethnography is an "autobiographical genre of writing and research" (Ellis and Bochner 2000, p. 739). It brings together ethnography and autobiography in ways that have evolved in a number of directions. Our particular interest is the directions offered by poststructuralist autoethnography (Gannon 2003, 2006; Moneypenny 2013; Moneypenny and Kotzé 2014). Poststructuralist autoethnography provides opportunities to experiment with different ways of writing the self, while recognising that personal narratives can always only be partial and incomplete (Jackson and Mazzei 2012). As the autoethnographic excerpts that follow illustrate, "the authority for the story begins with the body and memories of the autoethnographic writer at the scene of lived experience" (Gannon 2006, p. 475), and these are of necessity limited.

Foucault's general suggestion about writing might well be applied to the orientation taken in writing autoethnography: "I am an experimenter in the sense that I write in order to change myself and in order not to think the same thing as before" (2000, p. 240). Such writing has an ethical purpose, as Gannon explains:

> The purpose of writing is "nothing less than the shaping of the self" [Foucault 1997a, p. 211] through reflexive and imaginative attention to everyday lived experience and ethical principles for living. Writing the self produces transformation of the self and, potentially, of the world in local and particular contexts. (2006, p. 479)

This argument is in line with Michael White's (2000) caveat that in narrative therapy, a therapist does not know in advance of the therapy how a client's life should be lived. At the start of a research study, an autoethnographer does not know what new thoughts might become possible, what possibilities for just practice or for ethical subjectivity might emerge. Autoethnographic writing thus tends to emerge in a rhizomatic fashion—taking directions that cannot be predicted or known in advance. The research occurs in the process of writing, in bringing into dialogue self and culture.

As we turn now to Andrew's autoethnographic study (Kulasingham 2013), we pause again at the rhizome. We do not claim a linear relationship between autoethnography and therapy practice. Instead, we suggest that writing the self in dialogue with theory, ethics and culture provided a meaningful shaping of Andrew's therapeutic practice, his becoming. *Becoming* is the second Deleuzo-Guattarian concept that we employ in this chapter. It continues the metaphor of a rhizome's nonlinear growth and disrupts familiar understandings of linearity:

> A line of becoming is not defined by points it connects … on the contrary, it passes *between* points, it comes up through the middle … a line of becoming has neither beginning nor end, departure nor arrival, origin nor destination … A line of becoming has only a middle … (Deleuze and Guattari 1987, p. 293)

In writing here of Andrew's *becoming,* our focus is on a dialogue that is "always in process" between the self, ethics, professional practice and culture.

Andrew describes himself as a Malaysian-born Sri Lankan Tamil who immigrated with his immediate family to Aotearoa, New Zealand. As part of his Master of Counseling study at the University of Waikato, he used autoethnography to explore his relationship with three generations of women in his family: his mother, his wife and his daughter. Andrew hoped to reshape his contributions to relational practices, in this way becoming different from what he was before the conversations that took place as part of his research explorations. In order to include in these conversations his mother who had passed away—the focus of this chapter—Andrew invited his siblings to assist in researching moments of his mother's life story. The research conversations for his autoethnography produced many challenging and poignant moments. Listening to the narratives of the significant women in his life, researching theory and philosophies, Andrew revisited, reshaped and rewrote relational practices that produced movements and *becomings* in personal and professional relationships in expected and unexpected ways.

## Re-membering Practices in an Autoethnographic Study

Andrew's autoethnographic study drew on narrative therapy's remembering practices (White 1988, 2007; Hedtke 2003; Hedtke and Winslade 2004, 2005), reshaping these practices as a research method. Re-membering conversations are "reengagements with the history of one's relationships", with the purpose of revising the "memberships" one has with significant others in one's life (White 2007, p. 129). Andrew drew on re-membering practices in investigating his relationship with his deceased mother, Ranji. Through this work, he reclaimed his mother's membership of what narrative therapy calls his "club of life" (White 1988, 2007; Hedtke and Winslade 2004), in other words, those persons whose presence enhances well-being and supports what we ourselves care about and hope for in our lives.

Andrew remembers:

I had never spoken about the seven years of being separated from my mother, as I lacked the vocabulary to articulate the story. I never asked my mother the nagging question: why? Even after I returned to live with the family, we never discussed this. How could I discuss it? How could I ask her these questions that had been on my mind since being away? 'Mom, why did you send me away? How did you find it in your heart to do that? Could you not see it in my eyes? Didn't you hear me? Those teary eyes, those tight hugs when you said goodbye. They were saying only one thing. Don't leave me again. Take me home. Mom, why did you send me away?' How could I possibly ask these questions? I loved her and I knew she loved me. To talk about these things would bring up old hurts and risk altering this loving relationship built through the years.

The separation from his mother and siblings, following the sudden death of his father, had brought pain, confusion and a longing to belong, unspoken until Andrew began speaking the story in the Master of Counseling program. In conversations with family and friends, he asked why he was sent away for seven years to live with extended family in a town far away from his mother. Andrew revisited his relationship with his mother, Ranji, and told and retold the story of being separated from his mother as a child in research conversations with Elmarie and in conversation with other family members.

In one re-membering conversation, Andrew and his sister discussed the visits that their mother Ranji made to Andrew during his years away from her. Andrew learned that his mother knew how expectantly he awaited her visit. His sister said: "Mom knew you would be the first person to greet her at the door. You would hold her hand and never let it go". Ranji knew he was waiting for her, and she never disappointed him. Every visit kept the smouldering hope of reunion alive. Weingarten (2000, p. 8) speaks of hope as a verb, an active continuous practice, bringing "people together to work toward a preferred future". As his mother continued to work towards bringing him home, the visits ensured not just a continued relationship, but a "doing hope" (Weingarten 2010) of being together again one day.

The term "re-membering" was first used by Barbara Myerhoff, an anthropologist, who worked with elderly Jewish communities in California. The practice of re-membering refers to the reintroduction of members of one's life story and the performance of one's story to an audience who witness to one's identity claims. White (1997) reshaped the practice of "re-membering" in introducing it to narrative therapy, and developing the "club of life" metaphor (1988, 1997, 2007). First, rather than encouraging those who are grieving the loss of a loved one to gradually work towards accepting the loss by "saying goodbye", White (1988) proposed practices of "saying hullo again". "Saying hullo again" is an invitation to people who are grieving to maintain an ongoing relationship with the person who has passed on, by renewing the deceased's "membership of the club of life" (White 2007, p. 138). Second, White suggested that therapeutic re-membering conversations "encourage the development of notions of identity that emphasize the contributions that others make to our lives and to our understandings of self" (2007, p. 138).

We now turn to Andrew's autoethnography. The development of his study took a rhizomatic path, even though in this chapter, we resort to a linear telling of the story. Andrew came to understand the actions, dilemmas and decisions of his mother Ranji by tracing some of her journey as a Malaysian-born Sri Lankan Tamil woman. Ranji's life took many turns and we start with Andrew's writing of the silence and separation that shaped their relationship, even after she passed on.

## Writing Separation and Silence

Ranji left her dreams at the Sikamat cemetery. Widowed at 37, with four young children, her life became unbearably challenging. The two older boys were sent away as the extended family made decisions to help her to get back on her feet. Junior, the eldest, returned after one year, while Andrew, her third child, remained separated from her for seven years. However, she visited him every month. For seven years, every month, she boarded a bus from Seremban to Kajang on a

Saturday morning. In Kajang, she took another bus to the capital city, Kuala Lumpur, where Andrew lived. The four-hour trip to see her son did not seem too long to her. Always filled with anticipation, her life revolved around these monthly visits: month after month, year after year, one birthday after another, for seven years.

These seven years were difficult years for Andrew. His life revolved around the cycle of his mother's visits. He counted the days until the next visit. He stood at the door waiting for her, waiting to hug her. He was happiest on those weekends when she came to visit. She was kind and had a soothing voice. She always spoke gently to him. He could see in her eyes a mother's love. She loved him. It always seemed that the weekend would come to an end as soon as it began. She would leave him again. Why? He did not know. He cried a lot. Not in front of anyone. He could not. His aunt and uncle were kind enough to look after him. He was not their child. He could not cry in front of them. That would be ungrateful. His tears spoke a language he understood. Tears would say things he could not say. Each time his mother left, he wanted to say, "Please don't leave me again. Take me back with you". He could not say it, so he used the only language he knew—tears. Why would she not take him back? Why only him? His siblings were with her. Why was he sent away? Was something wrong with him? The questions were left unspoken and unanswered. Another monthly visit would come to an end. "Maybe next month", he would say to himself. "Maybe next month, she will take me home". Andrew and Ranji both carried the pain of the separation in silence… no questions, no explanations. However, Ranji visited Andrew … once a month for seven years. Ranji resisted the curious, evaluative gazes of bystanders, the spoken and unspoken pressures of cultural norms of marriage for the sake of "normality" or "sameness" and kept working, sometimes more than one job, to visit him once a month. She faced hardship, hard labour, poverty, overcrowded buses and tiring journeys to stay present in her son's life.

## Resembling a Family

The day finally came. In 1977, Ranji made arrangements to bring her son back home. It was not an ideal situation. Her landlord raised the rent beyond what she could afford. Ranji and her children moved into the spare room of the home of another relative who lived in the same town. Ranji brought Andrew back to live there with the family. For six months, they lived in a cramped room, five of them. Those were the worst times for Ranji and her children. The children experienced violence from male relatives, who took it upon themselves to discipline the children. Andrew's brother, Junior, bore the brunt of it. Ranji could not prevent it: she was silenced. She had no say. She was silenced by men, who were granted cultural and gendered rights over women's and children's lives.

From the in-between time of silence and separation, the rhizomatic growth of resembling a family became possible in 1977 as Andrew reunited with his family.

However, another silence, imposed by violence and intimidation, was brought about from within the extended family. This period was followed by another *becoming,* as Ranji emerged, from beneath patriarchal violence and displacement, as a homeowner.

## A Tiny Terraced House

The year 1978 would inscribe itself as a time of change in Ranji's life. With the support of a group of four women friends, she took a loan and purchased a small house. This was no easy feat. At 43, with no knowledge of property ownership, she embarked on a path she had never walked. She engaged a lawyer, filled out loan applications and went hunting for a suitable house, fuelled by the single passion to provide her children with a safe home.

Finally, she moved into her new home in Seremban—a tiny terraced house, linked to a row of houses that shared their side walls. Ranji now had new dreams. Her children's future was her dream. She was building a life for them, a life beyond a cycle of violence and poverty. The house was more than a shelter from the scorching sun and monsoon rain. It was a sanctuary. The violence and abuse ceased: Ranji distanced herself from relatives who had been abusive to the children. All four children were together again. She held multiple jobs to pay the mortgage and feed her four children. Ranji entered yet another facet of the economic machine of capitalism, this time as a homeowner submitting to the scrutiny of financial viability as a single woman, a mortgage and extended hours of labour to provide security and safety.

Ranji carefully planned family rituals and celebrations. Every New Year's morning, Ranji left a multi-page letter at the foot of each child's bed. In the letters, she acknowledged their achievements in the previous year and encouraged them with feedback on areas to work on in the coming year. Education was an important theme. She encouraged them to study hard. She wanted them to achieve their dreams. This was now her new dream. She was building a home in which her four children could build their dreams, a home that would catapult them out of a life of poverty into new horizons, new possibilities and new dreams.

Andrew, as son and his mother's executor, remembers:

The year before my mother died, she asked me if I could finalise the deed to the house as it was still in the land office. After two days of getting the run-around from one unit to another unit in the government department, I finally had the deed in my hands. I remember my mother's face when she held the deed in her hands. She hugged me. She then sat and stared at the deed for a long while. She could now write her will. This deed was more than a deed to her house. It embodied her legacy. My mother appointed me as the executor of her will and discussed the will with me before she died. She wanted the house to go to my sister to ensure that my sister never had to go through what she had gone through. Whatever circumstances my sister would face, she would have a house to keep her family together.

We draw attention to this deed for the tiny terraced house, linked to a row of houses that shared their side walls in Seremban, Malaysia. The deed represents connections and commitments. The piece of paper did not erase the marks of the hard labour, the struggle written on Ranji's body. Andrew and Ranji carried the memories, the marks on their bodies, and at the same time, they experienced the force of joy as their hands touched the deed, their eyes cherished the deed, their eyes met each other; and transformation, becoming, became possible.

## Autoethnography and Becoming

A process of *becoming* emerged on and from the pages of the autoethnographic dissertation and changed experience beyond those pages. Andrew's autoethnographic text both captures and produces these moments of rhizomatic becoming.

As a Malaysian-born Sri Lankan Tamil, a person in between multiple cultures, Andrew had many experiences that can be described as being positioned as "different-other". In his research, he positioned himself even more explicitly as in-between, moving even more overtly into being in the middle (see Deleuze and Guattari 1987). With this purpose in mind, he invited three generations of women to speak into his "becoming different" as he researched and wrote his autoethnography. In the next section, we call on the relational wisdom and learning that became possible through Andrew's autoethnography and how this became visible and grew into in his family therapy practice.

## Andrew as Family Therapist

They are crammed together around a small meeting table, a lawyer, a mother and a family therapist, Andrew. It is a small table in a small meeting room in the offices of a small legal firm in a provincial city in Aotearoa New Zealand. (Client names and identifying information have been changed.)

The lawyer has been appointed by the court to represent the two children in the family. The children are twins, a girl and a boy. The family came to the attention of the court when the boy reported physical violence at the hands of his father. In the ensuing intra-actions in which this mixed-race migrant family became caught up—intra-actions between a migrant father's child-discipline practices, and contemporary Western practices of care and protection—the force of New Zealand law removed both children from the parents and placed them with caregivers, for the children's protection. Subsequently, the father has secured work in another city. The mother lives alone in the family's rental home.

The interventions mandated for the family include a series of interactions between the family therapist and the family. There seems to be an assumption that the problem lies in the cultural practices of this migrant family. Andrew's first meeting with the family is intended to set up the mandated interventions. Subsequently, he meets with the parents on a number of occasions over several months to deliver a court-mandated parenting course. The father's absence from the last two meetings, due to his work in another city, provides further opportunities for Andrew to ask careful questions that once again clarify that the children's mother is not herself subjected to violence.

As mandated by the court, Andrew also meets with the children, individually and together, for therapy. For them, returning home has now become urgent: when it was proposed that they would be placed with caregivers, they expected this placement away from home to be for a few days, not months, as it has become. Despite their fondness for the caregivers with whom they have been placed, and their wish for their father to cease to use physical discipline on his son, the separation from their parents causes ongoing distress. Andrew purposely tells the children about how their parents have engaged in the parenting programme and how much their mother is looking forward to their return home.

The mother and Andrew arrive at today's meeting together. From the moment of entering the professional offices, Andrew notices the mother shrinking into herself. This is unlike her demeanour in therapy over recent weeks, but he knows that this is the first time she will meet an officer of the court without her husband present. In her husband's presence, she has always taken a culturally mandated second place. She has often been silent or silenced. He knows that her silence has been read by the court and by the care and protection systems as a submission that produces a failure to care and protect her children. But after twelve meetings with both parents together, and with the mother alone, Andrew knows that silence is more complex than this: for example, a mother's silence is described by Ohye (1998) as "eloquent and resonant" (p. 135). Andrew's understanding of the complexity of silence is a moment of rhizomatic thinking. This migrant mother is about to encounter a legal system that has separated her from her twins: it is hardly surprising that she may take a deferential position in the face of such authority. At the same time, in terms of considering what knowledge may be implicit within the act of refraining from speaking, Andrew holds both personal and professional knowledge of the multiple possible ways in which silence speaks. As he notices the mother shrinking into herself, Andrew recalls therapy conversations where she spoke clearly about parenting practices. He entered the meeting having assessed that the mother is now well positioned to protect her children in the context of the family.

The meeting has been called to advance the matter of the children returning home. Given that the father is no longer living in the family home, the children's return home appears to all involved to be the next step. But first the court requires the mother to take out a protection order against her husband (see http://www.justice.govt.nz/family-justice/domestic-violence/protection-order). The conditions of this order of the court require that the father, as respondent, does not contact the family, or engage in violence against them. The lawyer, on behalf of the court, advises the mother that this is the step she must take. The mother, Qui (identifying information changed), quietly refuses. This is the first time Andrew sees Qui step forward in this way beyond the therapy room. He recognises it as a big step for her in terms of culture/gender. But the lawyer repeats that the court requires her to take out a protection order to provide for the family's safety. Qui again quietly refuses. A stalemate arises.

Recognising the potential significance of the step Qui has taken in her refusal, Andrew asks her about her concerns and hesitation in taking out the order. Qui replies that she wants to keep the relationship with her husband and a protection order would get in the way of this hope. Andrew asks about her desire to be with her children and to protect them. Qui replies that she wants to ensure their safety, but she does not understand why she has to take out a protection order when it is her children who are to be kept safe. Her speaking this apparent contradiction creates a rhizomatic possibility. Andrew meets with contemplative silence the contradiction that becomes evident in her words. Andrew is not surprised to hear again that Qui is committed to her children, and he understands that whatever decisions are made here could have economic implications and have implications for a future reconciliation with her husband. In this silence—that responds to Qui's refusal to take out a protection order in her name, and the contradiction that becomes evident—space opens to hear her speaking as a becoming other than she was before. Her speaking is not the refusal of a woman required to take second place, but that of a migrant woman who is working to manage the complexities of competing responsibilities, seeking to make the best of the narrow discursive spaces in which her life is currently constituted. The emergence of the rhizome—in the space created by refusal and silence—has shifted the ground between the woman, the therapist and the lawyer.

Andrew asks Qui further about her hesitation and concerns, and she speaks of her desire to keep the family together while the children's father is away. She wants to protect the children and to also keep the possibility of a relationship with her husband alive. She emphasises her responsibility to protect her children, but at the same time, she explains that she wants the freedom for her husband to see her. She indicates a clear understanding that the court forbids him to see the children until he has met all the requirements set out by the court at the outset of this situation. Andrew again understands that Qui is seeking choices that will keep the family together. Qui makes a case for seeing her husband, while not advocating that he see the children. The terms of the protection order that the court requires her to take out do not make it possible for her to see her husband, and that means she cannot fulfil her hope of finding a way to keep the family together. Andrew turns to the lawyer and asks whether the legal system offers any other way forward, any way to protect the children while keeping open the possibility of the marital relationship's having a future.

At first, it appears that the stalemate will prevail. The lawyer expresses her concern for safety of the mother. Qui replies that she is not afraid of her husband. The lawyer asks Qui if she would call the police if there were problems. She says she would. She reports that she herself has not felt unsafe or afraid of her husband but that she has previously deferred to her husband's culturally mandated responsibility to discipline their son, including discipline by physical means. She says that her husband's departure to another city for work is his contribution to giving her and the children an opportunity to be a family together. A protection order preventing her husband from contact with her does not fit in with how this family is working things out. Qui is quietly dignified in her replies, in the face of the lawyer's gentle but insistently probing questions.

Again, in support of Qui's quiet persistence, Andrew asks the lawyer if there is any possible option that could allow Qui and the children to be together without a protection order in Qui's name. This question gives impetus to the rhizomatic possibilities that had been lingering as traces amidst the speaking, silence, people, documents, and furniture, in this small room. Up, through the middle, an unanticipated moment of becoming emerges, as the stalemate is broken and an alternative course of action becomes available. The decision is made that a protection order is to be taken out, not on behalf of the mother, but on behalf of the children. In this way, the court's requirements for protection are fulfilled, and simultaneously the mother's hope of caring for and protecting her children, and keeping her family together, is realised. This moment of becoming that emerges in the middle of things—in the midst of struggle, of the power of the law, of vulnerability, of professional responsibility, of lived experience of separations—is a becoming for all who are present, for the lawyer, for Qui and for Andrew, as therapist-in-relation.

## Narrow Discursive Spaces

At the start of this article, we signalled our interest in practices of therapy woven with the "more complex understanding of context, of multiplicity, and of social justice" that Dickerson (2014, p. 412) argues for. Migration is complex, and as Fraktman (1998) demonstrated, it is too easy to assume deficit as migrant families negotiate multiple cultures, economics, education, family practices and legal processes. As a family therapist, Andrew is also subject to the force of the law at the outset of the work with Qui and her family. At first, his own migrant status seems something of an impediment, in the narrow discursive space that appears to be available to him to engage with this family and to undertake court-mandated interventions, overseen by statutory authority. What can therapy do in the face of what this family is up against?

Taking this question to professional supervision, Andrew paid attention to this experience of a doubled marginalisation—on one hand the migrant family and on the other his position as a (migrant) therapist. In an outsider witnessing consultation with Kathie and his class peers, Andrew came to remove the brackets from the term "migrant" and to highlight this word as he retold what he was contributing to the multiplicity of this assemblage of family/court/child protection agency/school/lawyer, out of his own experiences of migration, of difference from the dominant culture in which he had become domiciled and from his professional expertise. What did his particular knowledges bring that was otherwise unavailable? What might that mean for this family? How might this whole assemblage come to benefit from the particularities of Andrew's professional contributions and multiple lived experiences? The witnessing conversations, out of which these questions emerged for Andrew, served as a means of rhizomatic becoming. In the account of his practice told and retold, Andrew emerged in the middle of, indeed pivotal to, what became possible for the family to do.

## Becoming Rhizome

Our story of the meeting between Qui, the lawyer and Andrew offers a glimpse of practices that emerged alongside this family. In the midst of legal/therapeutic processes, unpredicted becomings occurred, rhizomatic expressions of Andrew's own family life in his professional practice.

> [A rhizome] has no middle: no trunk. And it has no end: no leaves. It is always in the middle, always in process. There is no particular shape it has to take and no particular territory to which it is bound. It can connect from any part of itself to a tree, to the ground, to the fence, to other plants, to itself. (May 2005, p. 133)

In asking how Andrew's autoethnography and his lived experience were present in his family therapy practice, we find the explanatory force of the Deleuzo-Guattarian metaphor of the rhizome attractive. We do not argue that Andrew's therapy practice is a tree that grew from the roots of Andrew's childhood, through the trunk of his adult life, and the branches of his professional education. Rather, we suggest that, just like the rhizome, therapeutic practice has no centre; it is always in process. We do not claim that there is some linear causality between the self-writing and re-membering of the autoethnography and Andrew's therapeutic self and practice. Rather, these side-by-side stories—autoethnographic writing and professional practice with a family—illustrate a multi-directional, rhizomatic and multiple becoming.

The stories of mothers (Ranji and Qui) and their children meet in a network of random connections. All three children were removed from their family home in a moment of family crisis, and all three came to understand the care with which their mothers continued to work to parent them throughout this separation. Andrew positioned himself to learn from Ranji and her life, and what he learned emerged in unexpected ways as he met with Qui. He came to understand how both Ranji and Qui worked to produce small everyday practices (Coll et al. 1998) that resisted dominant and oppressive descriptions of women and mothers. For example, Ranji might have been expected to marry again, or to leave her son in a home where there were two parent figures, and Qui might have been expected to end her relationship with her husband to ensure protection for her children. But Ranji remained single and persevered in her visits to her son over seven years until she could bring him home, and Qui persisted in valuing her marriage relationship, working towards its continuance while safely mothering her son and daughter. Ranji took the bus to visit her son, she brought him home, she bought a house, she worked three jobs, she wrote letters, and she gifted the deed of her house to her daughter. Qui attended a parenting course, she maintained a home in the family's rental property, and she refused to sign a protection order that did not also protect what she valued. Ranji and Qui produced non-conformative mothering:

> We need not conform. Indeed, if our lives are to be interesting ones, capable of new feelings, new pleasures, new thoughts and experiences, we must not conform. Deleuze offers us a radically different way to approach living, and an attractive one, as long as we are ready to ask anew what it is to be *us* and what it is to be *living*. (May 2005, p. 25)

Both Ranji and Qui showed Andrew what not conforming might do. Andrew learned to read these actions as possibilities for ethical living. He brought patience, observation, refined inquiry and openness to being taught by women—to the autoethography, to the therapy and to this current writing.

Particularly poignant as we write now is that without their having shared a physical meeting, the lives of Ranji and Qui come together in processes of becoming through the ways they forged relationships with two particular legal documents. Significant personal and social and political meaning is invested in these documents, which produced significant becomings for both women and both families, *becomings* that were emergences not end points. A deed of ownership signifies Ranji's refusal to conform to her culture/time, and how hard she worked, over time, for what was important to her in her life as a mother and as her legacy. The protection order on behalf of her children signifies Qui's refusal to conform to the dominant practices in her country of migration, at the same time as she used the law to provide protection for her children. Andrew wrote in his autoethnography that the title deed meant more than a deed for a house: it was Ranji's legacy. But he could not have predicted the ways in which Ranji's legacy would also be expressed through his responses to Qui's calm insistence that a protection order in her name was not the way forward. Both women, Ranji and Qui, came to hold legal documents in their hands, and in both situations, the documents expressed more than the legal phrases could imagine. They held in their hands legal documents that expressed what they cared deeply about.

## Conclusion

This chapter has made a beginning in exploring the emergence of therapy practice in rhizomatic relationship with lived experience, re-membered through autoethnographic research. Autoethnography writes the self in relationship with culture, exploring a culture or indeed several cultures through a retelling of one's relationships with others and with the practices of one's culture. This is a story of professional education and professional practice, a rhizomatic telling of becoming therapist, an acknowledgement of the privilege of learning for the three of us who have come to write this work together. This telling is made possible only through the gifts of knowing something of the lives of Ranji and Qui.

> The past is never closed, never finished once and for all, but there is no taking it back, setting time aright, putting the world back on its axis. There is no erasure finally. The trace of all reconfigurings are written into the enfolded materialisations of what was/is/to-come. Time can't be fixed. To address the past (and future), … is not to entertain or reconstruct some narrative of the way it was, but to respond, to be responsible, to take responsibility for that which we inherit (from the past and the future), for the entangled relationalities of inheritance that 'we' are, to acknowledge and be responsive to the noncomtemporaneity of the present, to put oneself at risk, to risk oneself …. (Barad 2010, p. 264).

## References


Barad, K. (2010). Quantum entanglements and hauntological relations of inheritance: Dis/continuities, spacetime enfoldings, and justice-to come. *Derrida Today, 3*(2), 240–268.

Coll, C. G., Surrey, J., & Weingarten, K. (Eds.). (1998). *Mothering against the odds: Diverse voices of contemporary mothers*. New York: Guilford Press.

Conley, V. (2006). Borderlines. In I. Buchanon & A. Parr (Eds.), *Deleuze and the contemporary world* (pp. 95–107). Edinburgh, United Kingdom: Edinburgh University Press.

Deleuze, G. & Guattari, F. (1987). *A thousand plateaus: Capitalism and schizophrenia.* (B. Massumi, Trans.). Minneapolis, MN: University of Minnesota Press.

Dickerson, V. (2014). The advance of poststructuralism and its influence on Family Therapy. *Family Process, 53*(3), 410–414.

Ellis, C., & Bochner, A. (2000). Autoethnography, personal narrative, reflexivity: Research as subject. In N. Denzin & Y. Lincoln (Eds.), *Handbook of Qualitative Research* (2nd ed., pp. 733–768). Thousand Oaks, CA: Sage.

Foucault, M. (1997). The ethics of the concern of the self as a practice of freedom. In P. Rabinow (Ed.), Michel Foucault. Ethics: Essential works of Foucault 1954–1984, Vol 1. (R. Hurley & others Trans.). New York, NY: New York Press.

Foucault, M. (2000). Interview with Michel Foucault. In J. D. Faubion (Ed.), *Power: Essential works of Foucault 1954–1984* (Vol. 3, pp. 239–297). New York, NY: New York Press.

Fraktman, M. (1998). Immigrant mothers: What makes them high risk? In C. Coll, J. Surrey, & K. Weingarten (Eds.), *Mothering against the odds: Diverse voices of contemporary mothers* (pp. 85–107). New York, NY: Guilford Press.

Gannon, S. (2003). Flesh and text: Poststructural theory and writing research. Unpublished Doctoral thesis, James Cook University, Townsville, Australia.

Gannon, S. (2006). The (Im)possibilities of writing the self-writing: French poststructural theory and autoethnography. *Cultural Studies,critical Methodologies, 6,* 474–495.

Hedtke, L. (2003). The origami of remembering. *International Journal of Narrative Therapy and Community Work, 4*, 51–62.

Hedtke, L., & Winslade, J. (2004). *Re-membering lives. Conversations with the dying and the bereaved.* Amityville, NY: Baywood.

Hedtke, L., & Winslade, J. (2005). The use of the subjunctive in re-membering conversations with those who are grieving. *OMEGA, 50*(3), 197–215.

Jackson, A. Y., & Mazzei, L. (2012). *Thinking with theory in qualitative research: Viewing data across multiple perspectives*. London, United Kingdom: Routledge.

Kulasingham, A. (2013). Re-authoring family relationships: An Autoethnographic study on dialogical conversations and repositioning, Unpublished M Couns dissertation, University of Waikato, New Zealand.

May, T. (2005). *Gilles Deleuze. An introduction.* Cambridge, United Kingdom: Cambridge University Press.

Moneypenny, P. (2013). A poststructural autoethnography: Self as event. Unpublished Master's thesis. University of Waikato, Hamilton, New Zealand.
Moneypenny, P., & Kotzé, E. (2014). "I cannot see my way clear, I cannot see the blackboard": Deconstructing personal failure stories. *New Zealand Journal of Counselling, 34*(1), 37–52.
Ohye, B. (1998). Safeguarding wordless voice in a world of words. In C. Coll, J. Surrey, & K. Weingarten (Eds.), *Mothering against the odds: Diverse voices of contemporary mothers* (pp. 134–150). New York, NY: Guilford Press.
Weingarten, K. (2000). Witnessing, wonder, and hope. *Family Process, 39*(4), 389–402.
Weingarten, K. (2010). Reasonable hope: Construct, clinical applications, and supports. *Family Process, 49*(1), 5–25.
White, M. (1988). Saying hullo again: The incorporation of the lost relationship in the resolution of grief. *Dulwich Centre Newsletter, 3*, 7–11.
White, M. (1991). Deconstruction and therapy. *Dulwich Centre Newsletter, 3*, 121–151.
White, M. (1997). *Narratives of therapists' lives*. Adelaide, Australia: Dulwich Centre Publications.
White, M. (2000). *Reflections on narrative practice. Essays and interviews*. Adelaide, Australia: Dulwich Centre Publications.
White, M. (2007). *Maps of narrative practice*. New York, NY: Norton.
White, M., & Epston, D. (1990). *Narrative means to therapeutic ends*. New York, NY: Norton.
Winslade, J. (2009). Tracing lines of flight: Implications of the work of Gilles Deleuze for narrative practice. *Family Process, 4*(3), 332–346.

# Constructing Matrilineal Connections in a Remembering Conversation

**Lorraine Hedtke**

**Abstract** People often search for meaning to soothe the pain of grief. Some turn to religious doctrine or secular rituals, others toward counseling. Some may connect to ancestral stories to find genealogical meaning for their own lives. Each of these quests may be aided by counseling conversations. Death particularly challenges the meanings of a relationship. This chapter will showcase the use of "remembering conversations" with a woman whose mother had recently died. Rather than finding personal meaning in her own individuality, she is comforted by finding it in a renewed sense of lineage, connecting meaning to her mother, grandmother, and her daughter. By crafting questions that focus on what remains following the death of a loved one, a counselor can assist the bereaved to connect multigenerational meaning with narrative legacies. These stories can infuse the relationship between the living and the dead, often affirming familial connections, with strength and vitality. The transcript of a narrative counseling session will be featured along with contextualization of the practices.

When a person who matters dies, the living are left with a desire to make sense of events. Circumstances dictate they make meaning of what has happened, accounting for the existential questions of life and death, but also for the changes in relationship. It is simply not good enough to create a premature good-bye or insist that people find closure, as these undermine the beauty that can be created. A bereaved person often seeks to fill a sense of yearning for the deceased. This desire lies behind the continuing bonds idea (Klass, Silverman & Nickman, 1996) that has been popular in recent grief psychology (Hagman 2001).

The span of my professional career has centered on helping those who are dying and those who are living with grief to make sense of these events. The counseling support, as well as the professional teaching, I am involved in, has challenged the individual paradigm, often found in conventional grief psychology. The practices I have embodied support relationships, with the living and not, to bring forward

L. Hedtke (✉)
California State University, San Bernardino, CA, USA
e-mail: lorrainehedtke@gmail.com



V. Dickerson (ed.), *Poststructural and Narrative Thinking in Family Therapy*, AFTA SpringerBriefs in Family Therapy, DOI 10.1007/978-3-319-31490-7_4

stories of strength and agency, often in the face of tremendous emotional distress and injustice.

Undercurrents in conventional grief psychology models have, at times, unwittingly led to the invisibilizing of the deceased, including requirements for a final good-bye and the letting go of relationship. This omission not only obscures the life of the deceased person, but also inflicts unnecessary pain upon the immediate family and friends, as well as all possible future connections. As the reader will find, the practice of remembering opposes acts that sever relational connections. In the particular story that follows, the matriarchal knowledges that can be willed to future generations is doubly threatened by the discounting of women's knowledge in patriarchal practices (Belenky et al. 1986; Goldberger et al. 1996). These domains of power and privilege follow people to the grave where some lives are considered grievable, while others are not (Butler 2004).

Bringing to life a storied connection with the deceased becomes a political act that refuses relegation of a relationship to oblivion and in the process refuses the dominating influence of patriarchal discourse. Remembering is more than a quaint cultural practice or the private experience of continuing a bond. It becomes a platform for making a person's life visible and encourages projects that mattered to the deceased to be taken up by those who continue to live. In the process, the bereaved can find comfort and the deceased can be given a visible and just tribute for what they have stood for. Remembering affirms that a bond be continued, in this instance, through generations of women who have come before and those yet to be born to honor matrilineal knowledge.

Rather than concentrating on continuing bonds as an empirical description of what people do, the aim of this chapter is to illustrate the therapeutic use of this idea. When appropriately supported, the bereaved can find a renewed and rich ongoing connection with the deceased person that they continue to care about. This chapter explores how to facilitate such a rich, ongoing connection between the living and dead through the crafting of questions. Rather than thinking of death and grief as only an individual event, I will showcase the practice implications of addressing the despair of grief by thinking in relational terms and multigenerational legacies.

Many models of bereavement have been focused on the individual's internal process of recovery, omitting the familial structure, support, and changes (Nadeau 1998). It could even be said that grief is always an event that is shaped by the family structures, rituals, and meanings (ibid). The living continue to make sense of their grief in direct relation to the intricate patterns of interaction and relational knowledge of the constructs of the relationship that was, and the implications of the relationship to be (ibid).

This chapter will introduce "remembering practices," a narrative approach to therapeutic conversation that transcends the barriers between the living and the dead (Hedtke 2012b; Hedtke and Winslade 2004; White 1989, 2007). These conversations build a narrative legacy into the bereaved person's identity through transfusing the stories, strength, and love between generations. The thinking behind remembering conversations supports not only a narrative perspective but also is closely aligned with a family systems approach (Nadeau 1998), incorporating the relational threads between people's stories that create substance. Remembering generates vitality and helps craft a way forward in which the bereaved need not exclusively carry the burden of grief, as is often the case in individual grief models. If we hold to a postmodern view of identity, meanings are formed in pliable social networks and not by isolated individuals (Gergen 1991, 2000). The responses to grief thus created can uphold the importance of multigenerational family ties.

To illustrate remembering practices, this chapter highlights a transcribed conversation between myself and Megan and her mother Paula.[1]

My meeting with Megan was not the first conversation we had had about her mom. I had spoken with her mother, Paula, alone once before and once together with Megan. The conversation used here took place just three weeks after Paula's death. Paula had been ill for fourteen months with an aggressive cancer and had undergone many challenging medical procedures. This conversation also coincided with the early part of Megan's pregnancy, news of which she had shared with her mother before her passing. This grandchild was to be the first for Paula. These circumstances served as backdrop to a grief conversation that aimed to alleviate suffering (Attig 2001; Hedtke 2012a) and to uphold matriarchal knowledges that have, at times, been invisibilized in family therapy (McGoldrick 2004; Walsh and Scheinkman 1991; Hare-Mustin 1991).

However, before remembering can be described, a brief review of the dominant grief psychology is required which will contrast with a relational, narrative approach to grief.

## A Brief Review of Grief Psychology

Since Freud (1957), grief has been thought to reside within a person's psyche as an individual pathology (Hagman 2001; Walter 1999). Grief has been diagnosed as a collection of somatic symptoms (Lindemann 1944) that required a prescribed series of tasks to resolve (Worden 1991, 2009). Modern grief psychology has sought an emotional exorcism, or "decathexis" (Freud 1957) of emotional traces of connection with the deceased person. Counselors have guided people toward "an appropriate good-bye" (Worden's fourth and final task 1991, p. 38). Worden's later text softened this task to "finding an enduring connection with the deceased" (2009, p. 50), but the arc of his theory still reflects Freud's requirement to relinquish ties. Worden's third task, "adjusting to the world without the deceased" (2009, p. xiii), reflects this. The gold standard has been "acceptance" of death (Kübler-Ross 1969) and completing unfinished business. Absence of acceptance has been regarded as

[1]Megan Swanek gave permission for her name and this conversation to be published here. Her mother, Paula, and her father and brother also gave express permission to speak about and write about our conversations.

abnormal denial of the (physical) reality of death. Subsequent models have required further specific capitulations to the dominant psychology of grief and death.

Parkes states that "pangs of grief" (1972 p. 39) occur while the bereaved are adjusting to the reality of death but are short-lived. Bowlby (1969, 1973) suggested grief resulted from the rupturing of attachment. The task, according to Worden (1991), is to embrace the emotional pain and to "reinvest back into life" (p. 38) after processing the pain of grief (2009, p. 43).

Conventional practice has focused on "letting go," "moving on," finding "closure," and artificially separating the living from the dead through increasing emotional distance. Separating a deceased person from the living can actually be cruel when it exacerbates the sense of loss. By contrast, a different kind of conversation might entail appreciating what was important to the deceased. To this end, another approach to grief counseling is needed—one that affirms the best of what relationships have to offer (Hedtke 2001; Hedtke and Winslade 2004) and is supported by a growing body of research which indicates that meanings are made in a social and familial context, rooted in multigenerational legacies (Neimeyer 2001; Neimeyer et al. 2014; Walsh and McGoldrick 2004).

## Remembering Practices

Born out of social constructionism and narrative practice (White 2007), remembering conversations shift how we speak about the deceased (Hedtke and Winslade 2004; Myerhoff 1978, 1982, 2007). Narrative grief counseling does not require a solely individual perspective. Nor are the bereaved encouraged to excise the deceased person from memory or to reach a stage of acceptance of the loss. Instead, it focuses on the reincorporation of memories and on embracing the rich legacies found within families. Stories of hardships endured are often told and the teachings and values of the deceased are celebrated, long after the moment of death.

If a person's stories do not die with the death of the body, we are free to resurrect stories, retell, and reincorporate them into the lives of the living. Remembering expands understanding of time beyond a linear construction in which the deceased are relegated to the past, and instead generates clues to a relational future where a person's legacy can be shaped through posthumous accountability and care of the deceased person(s) stories. While some might see these claims as fanciful delusions, those that participate in these conversations report feelings of comfort (Hedtke 2012b).

Remembering conversations select stories from the deceased's life that might be useful to retain for the living. Finishing unfinished business becomes unnecessary, when we affirm the importance of ongoing relationship (Attig 2001). The relationship between the bereaved and the deceased morphs into something new, guided by the recollected words of the deceased.

However, in order to sift through which relational aspects may be useful, the deceased require an introduction (Hedtke 2012a). Counselors need to know who the deceased person was, what made them unique, what hobbies, work, or joys they invested in, and what was precious about them. Introduction is more than social formality. It may also alert the counselor to relationships that might be troubled or abusive. If so, a counselor would need to exercise care about whether a relationship should be reinstated. This chapter will not explore how to craft conversations in the face of abuse or traumatic death, as this emphasis can be found elsewhere (Hedtke 2012a). The transcribed excerpts with Megan illustrate how a remembering conversation can benefit a positive relationship in which the desire to include the deceased in the lives of the living already exists.

| | |
|---|---|
| Lorraine | Megan, can I get a sense of your mom? For those who don't know Paula. How would you introduce her? |
| Megan | She's the happiest, most carefree, easygoing person I've ever met. She can have fun doing anything - the grocery store, thrift store. |
| L | So, easygoing, appreciated a good joke, was happy doing just about anything. Yes? |
| M | Uh huh. Because she was so easygoing and sweet and kind, I never realized she was a strong person. She just had this quiet strength. She never complained. |
| L | So what's your best guess about how she was able to maintain that non-complaining stance during hard times, like with the cancer treatment? What did she call on to do that? |
| M | It's incredible to me. I just know that was how she lived her life. Even when it was really tested, she maintained strength and a non-complaining way. |
| L | So what's it like for you knowing that your mom was consistent? That before cancer, and during cancer, she was a woman who didn't complain, was strong, had things to look forward to, enjoyed laughing? |
| M | It's the best feeling in the world. I knew what to expect with her. It allowed me to be much more open, because she loved and accepted everything about me. |

Introducing sets the stage for a different kind of approach to grief psychology (Hedtke 2012a). It assumes from the beginning that the deceased continues to matter and the bereaved want to be accountable to the relationship. When psychology and medicine focus on the internal states of a grieving individual, this focus is left behind. Megan is asked to immediately call forward what is unique in their relationship. Through this, the counselor not only gets a sense of Paula, but also of what is noteworthy in Megan's life. Megan can invoke her mother's strength or humor to respond to her own life challenges. They can become valued attributes that guide Megan, while keeping her connected to her mother's abilities.

## The Theory Behind the Practice of Remembering

Remembering shifts how we think of identity and grief. The term, "re-membering,"[2] was coined by the anthropologist, Myerhoff (1978, 1982), to describe her community work with elderly Jewish people in Southern California in the 1970s and 1980s. Following the death of a community member, Myerhoff observed how, in the telling of the deceased person's stories, others gained a renewed sense of agency (Myerhoff 1978, 1982, 2007). According to Myerhoff, remembering is not passive or solitary, but the active conjuring of a person's importance for personal, and sometimes political, meanings.

Remembering[3] conversations are a springboard into relationship with a deceased person that transcend time and space. We are not bound by the limits of biology or theology as we invoke the "voice" and stories of the dead (Hedtke and Winslade 2005). We are free to speak the deceased into existence (Davies 1991) to establish renewed connection with them after their death.

Remembering offers Megan a new kind of continued relationship with Paula, albeit with different kinds of interaction, but a relationship nonetheless. It forms the basis for a future, where Paula's values and teachings continue to matter to Megan and to provide solace against the pain of grief. Remembering Paula helps Megan reincorporate her mother's stories into her own life. These stories pluck from the many possible versions to remember, what is most usable and sustaining.

| | |
|---|---|
| Lorraine | As you reflect on the last couple of months, what stands out that she's taught you? |
| Megan | That I need to not sweat the small stuff and not get upset with work situations, or drama with other family members. No matter how bad things are, there are always things to be grateful for. Even towards the end of her life, she was grateful that we were around her, that she could enjoy a cup of tea. It's just such a reminder that I don't want to get caught up in parts of life that down the road you're not going to remember. |
| L | You said something last time we spoke, about how she was teaching you about dying. You said you were doing better with being frightened about death, because she was teaching you. |
| M | My whole life, that's been my biggest fear. The time and energy I spent worrying about what it would be like to lose a parent! Although I'd give anything to have her here, it wasn't as bad as I thought. A big part of that is because of how she handled it. |
| L | Your biggest fear was of her death, is that right? |

---

[2]Myerhoff wrote about the term with a hyphen to separate the *RE* and membering to indicate the reinvestment of belonging to a group before, and after, death occurs. It is the constant reinclusion of a person's stories infused into a larger group, or what Michael White referred to a "Membership Club."

[3]For ease of reading, the hyphen will be assumed rather than written in this chapter.

M You know, if she had been questioning, "Why me?" or been upset and despondent it probably would have been worse. I feel like I can go through anything in life now, because I've been through that. It was hard seeing her decline and thinking, "I should have had twenty more years." What makes me feel better is knowing the time I've had with her was a gift.

L Since her passing, I know it's only been a few weeks, have you had a sense of those blessings continuing? Where have you noticed her calmness and her patience continuing with you?

M Yes, I ask myself what she would do in a situation.

L How is this for you?

M I will talk to her too and try to think of what she would say, give me advice, and use that to get through.

L When you do that, when you've been asking her questions, what is the effect of that for you?

Remembering picks up on the threads of relationship and sews them into a befitting meaning. The focus shifts from what was lost to what continues to be viable. Stories can embellish memories in order to find an ongoing voice for the deceased person. Often this person's "voice" can be invoked to act as guide through challenging terrain. For example, Megan explains how "listening" to her mother's advice is helpful.

Paula does not obviously speak with Megan. Nor does Meagan actually listen to her mother, other than perhaps a recording. Remembering draws upon memories to conjure Paula's presence in her preferences for how Megan should address hardships. These conversations are at first virtual but become actualized (Deleuze and Parnet 2002) as a basis for action.

As the conversation continues, Megan develops more of a sense of her mother's posthumous influence in her daily life. It is not unlike when Paula was alive and we are engaged in a family dialogue in which everyone's voice continues to matter and has the possibility of influencing others. Had the conversation focused on Megan's internal feeling state of loss, or encouraged her to move on from her mother's life lessons, it would cut Megan off from critical relational resources and not reflect how families form meaning, before and after a death (Nadeau 1998). Reconnecting her to her mother's stories and life lessons helps Megan to find her way as a newly bereaved woman and a soon-to-be young mother.

Megan I'd like to be able to recall her voice more still, but when I even just pause to think about her, it changes my behavior. It would be easy for me to miss this pause between being newly pregnant and just having lost her. There are situations where I could get really upset about something, or get upset with my husband. If I just pause and think, "What would she do?" it helps. It can change the way I react to a situation.

Lorraine How does it change the way that you react?

M Stopping and asking what mom would do helps me say, "This is not something that's going to be a big deal in five years." I don't need to overreact and be angry.

## Folds, Landscapes of Meaning, and Landscapes of Action

It is not enough to ask about a deceased person's voice. Remembering is, as Myerhoff (1982) wrote, more than the "fragmentary flickerings" (p. 111) of memories passively floating by. Remembering is the active development of a relationship that sustains and grows over time. Achieving this requires the crafting of a conversation that ebbs and flows between what Bruner (1986) spoke of as landscapes of action (the events that shape a narrative plot) and landscapes of meaning (the themes and values that give the plot depth). Weaving the two together develops a story pulsing with vitality. This bimodal conversation pattern is different from a dual-track model of bereavement (Stroebe and Schut 2001) that suggests a simultaneous letting go and reincorporation of the deceased person. Rather, a narrative model enlists plot developments alongside identity punctuation to create rich descriptions between the living and dead, where the dead continue to have an important role in the family.

As a counselor develops narrative remembering conversations, it is important to not only ask landscape-of-action questions as this produces a lopsided conversation, one without reflection about its significance resulting in shallow, meaningless narratives. Conversely, only asking reflective questions about meaning invites the potential for profound stuckness. Alternating between action and meaning, however, generates a rich narrative. Not only do the deceased have a say in the construction of the future actions of the living, but this say creates substantive meanings.

The layering, or folding of stories in on themselves, permeates remembering practices (Hedtke 2014; White 2007). Questions invite the telling of what happened in a linked series of events. Landscape-of-action questions invite Megan to situate her mother in her life but are only half of what is needed to generate a well-formed narrative. The other half involves reflecting on what such events mean and how this anchors Paula as continuing to be important in the family. This inquiry cements what would otherwise remain easily forgotten or could be intentionally overlooked in individually based counseling practices. Through this, reflexive generating of signification is formed as a newly folded crease in their relationship, connecting simple actions with meanings.

The advantage of thinking in terms of dual landscapes is that each fold (Deleuze's 1993, term) is like a switchback in a path that wends its way up a mountain. There are repeated opportunities to incorporate discrete aspects of relationship into the narrative. Each turn opens to new vistas, but there is still an upward motion in the apparent backtracking. We might even say the living become the eyes and ears of the dead, and the dead live on through stories told on their behalf.

Lorraine Do you have times or places where you think about her more often? [*Landscape of action*]

Megan I've been finding I think about her constantly.

L In what ways? [*Landscape of action*]

M All day, every day. It's pretty tough at night - I've been not sleeping well. And I'll wake from two in the morning until four-thirty and second-guess myself and think about the last few months that were tough for her. Whenever I start doing that, I try and go back to a vacation we took together.

L I see.

M I went to her remembrance mass. We were praying and I imagined reaching up and hugging her. And I did feel that at that time. I don't want to overuse it [the sense of being hugged], so I'm afraid to close my eyes and imagine hugging her again.

L So what would happen if you grabbed that sense of hugging her? [*landscape of meaning*]

M Oh, it gives me chills, and it feels really warming.

L So where was it that you felt this? [*Landscape of action*]

M In church.

L When you were at church, you were imagining connecting with her in heaven[4]? [*Landscape of action*]

M I was reaching up, and she was reaching down, and gave me a hug.

L The warming sensation – did it stay with you? [*Landscape of action*]

M Yeah, for a while after. I just felt calm. I felt I had been given a hug by her.

L Is that how her hugs felt in life? [*Landscape of action*]

M There are so many photos where we were hugging each other.

L Yeah. So tell me more about this hug from heaven? Where did she hold you when she was hugging you from heaven? [*Landscape of action*]

M Around my shoulders; around my back.

L Did your arms reach all the way around? [*Landscape of action*]

M Yes.

L What do you think it would mean for her, to hug you from heaven? [*landscape of meaning*]

M She said if she could find a way, or do something, she would. It would make her feel good to hug me. She loved taking care of people, and comforting people, and so she would know she had comforted me.

Moving between the dual landscapes builds the feeling of being hugged. It folds throwaway comments into the story and renders them sustaining and comforting. It affirms Paula's life as a mother who cares enough about her daughter to send a hug

[4]Megan had previously used this term when locating a sense of her mother. I did not suggest a religious metaphor that might not be her preferred way of thinking about afterlife.

from heaven. A posthumous intention, expressed in response to a subjunctive question (What would it mean to her?), is grafted onto Megan's stories. Megan's story is relationally positioned in response to who her mother has been, and continues to be.

Megan The last words she said to my father were, "Thank you," because he had given her a drink.

Lorraine Does it have meaning for you that those were the words, as opposed to anything else?

M Yeah, it shows how appreciative she was. For anything and everything.

In such a simple thankful statement, Megan again folds her mother's appreciative ways into her future story of Paula. Whenever Megan herself is appreciative, she can now connect with her mother's legacy.

## Relational Remembering

Grief counseling is always about at least two people, the living person and the person who has died (Hedtke 2012a). In a sense then, a remembering conversation is always a family conversation, even when it is only with one living person. There are always others' stories and legacies that shape and infuse the conversation. Remembering conversations weave stories and events into future legacies, not only for the bereaved, but also for future stakeholders, that is, for family members, as well as others in larger communities, who have yet to meet the deceased person.

Megan and her mother spoke about the art of crocheting as metaphorically intertwining them together. Paula had explained to me before her death that crocheting and knitting were skills that all the women in her family knew. Paula's mother's mother had taught her to crochet. It was an action that connected the women together in one legacy, and it was what Paula hoped Megan would teach her children some day. She hoped that Megan too would take up crocheting and "it would calm her and teach her patience."

Lorraine Your mom told me she was hoping there would be a place for crochet in your life. Not just because of making 'blankies'. Do you have a sense of what she was hoping for?

Megan Yeah, if I were stressed or worried, it would bring me into the present, by using my hands and creating something.

Here is an opportunity for multigenerational connections to shape Megan's experience. Crocheting establishes interlocking loops that take on healing qualities, when we thread them between Megan and Paula and capitalize on Paula's hopes for her daughter to have a calm and happy life. It is also an opportunity to take a stand against patriarchal assumptions that have devalued women's ways of knowing in life and in grief (Hare-Mustin and Marecek 1990).

| | |
|---|---|
| Lorraine | Let's imagine you get up at two in the morning. It's one of the nights where you're not sleeping, and you try crocheting, what would it be like to do something your mother taught you? |
| Megan | I'd feel closer to her, because she did that ever since she was a child right up until the end. |
| L | If she knew that you were crocheting as a calming mechanism, what would she say about that? |
| M | She'd be happy that she had given me a tool to feel better. |
| L | If you were crocheting, would you weave her into what you were making? |
| M | Yeah. |

## Remembering and Future Generations

Remembering conversations intend to help bereaved people find stories of strength at times of great pain. Such conversations seek out small acts and give the deceased's words an ongoing audience. The audience can be made of people the deceased person knew but can also be enlarged by the addition of people the deceased is introduced to. In this way, the deceased person's life is not over, as her stories and values continue to hold meaning for future generations.

Megan can keep her mother's stories viable through telling them to her husband and friends. She can share stories of her mother with her father and brother to honor Paula's place in their family. She can also imagine introducing Paula to her yet unborn daughter or any other future children. All of these actions honor the importance of Paula in the family system, even after death.

| | |
|---|---|
| Lorraine | If you were making baby booties for example and you were saying, "Oh, this is a place where me and my mom connect", how would that then be translated into the baby bootie? |
| Megan | It would be much more meaningful. The thoughts and the memories of us would be in there. There's a baby blanket that I'm almost finished that I started right after she was diagnosed and I thought about that. That it was with me through this last year, because I took it one time when we went to San Francisco. I was crocheting and she was crocheting. That blanket went on our journey. And those booties, if I'm feeling connected to her, then they're not just made out of regular yarn. |

The simplicity of crocheting a baby blanket or booties becomes the vessel for meaning, not only between Megan and her mother. It is the linking object (Vickio 1999) that also travels across distance and through time connecting Megan to her matrilineal lineage. In this way, what seems to be an "individual" counseling session becomes a something much more, where Megan is connected to a genealogy of female knowing.

| | |
|---|---|
| Megan | There's stories and memories and love in them [the baby booties]. |
| Lorraine | Stories and memories and love given to you by your mom? |
| M | Yeah and gifted from her mom and her grandma to her as well. |
| L | Is this connection actually a much longer lineage than just about you and Paula? Is it a lineage that connects her to her mother and then your grandmother to her mother too? So is it like you're the fourth generation of crocheters? |
| M | That we know of. Probably more. |

This piece of conversation brings into focus years of crocheting skill that have been passed down. For each person, it has had meaning about their place in this family and perhaps carried stories of patience and calmness. As Megan reflects, it is like holding a precious artifact. But it is not an artifact with a singular meaning but becomes a portal linking lives together. Its meaning can continue to grow and take shape. Historical time can be both collapsed into the present and expanded into the future, as Megan imagines the gifts this artifact will offer her daughter.

| | |
|---|---|
| Lorraine | Let's say you make these amazing little baby booties, and we have four generations, at least, of women who have had an experience of love through crocheting? |
| Megan | [*nodding*], Yeah. |
| Lorraine | What's it going to be like for your baby to wear those baby booties? |
| Megan | I'd like to think that wearing them, she'd feel warmer and feel loved, because they were made from love and with a connection to my mom. |
| Lorraine | How can you have a sense of certainty about that? |
| Megan | I do have a sense of certainty about that. They're definitely more meaningful. They definitely are filled with more love and time. |
| Lorraine | If you tell your daughter, let's say you save the baby booties, and when she's five, or ten, or fifteen years old, you tell her the story about how she wore these baby booties that you imagined had the love of all these women channeled into that yarn, what difference would you hope that would make for your child? |
| Megan | She would know that they did, because I would be making them with the craft that I was taught, and that she will be taught. But also the connection I feel to my mom and my daughter, while I'm making them. So with that explanation, she would feel love from generations of women. |

The folds of the conversation traverse time and space. Each fold of action and meaning produces a future history that enlivens generational connections, lessening the pain of grief. It is what Lambert (2002–2003) suggests as "extending biographies," as the stories of the ancestors are assimilated into the lives of the living and carried into a new future.

Lorraine As you tell your daughter of this connection to her grandmother and how her grandmother loves her, how does that settle for you Megan?

Megan My mom loves the baby. She got to hear the news that we were pregnant, a few times. Before that, she had told me, "I'm going to hold that baby." And so I know she already loves her.

The conversation can move vertically through time to fold in multigenerational attributes and stories. It also moves horizontally between people who share a love of Paula. Adding people from previous generations and from the present solidifies Paula's place in her posthumous identity.

Lorraine Would we want to bridge bits of this story with others? Because won't your husband, your brother, and your father and others also introduce the stories of your mom to your baby?

Megan Yes. Stories, photos, her voice. I want our child to know her, because it enhances her life to know about her grandmother.

L What in particular do you want your daughter knowing about Paula?

M I want her to know how kind and patient and happy she was. I want her to see that in me and to know that it definitely came from my mom.

Grief has the power to gut a person's life and make everyday events challenging. Remembering offers antidote to this in that stories are intentionally garnered for strength.

Lorraine Every day that you connect with your mom or think about her, are those places where you are living what she gave you?

Megan Yeah. I guess I am [*pause*]. I didn't think about it that way, but I am.

L What's that like?

M It feels really good. At night when things are tough and I'm thinking, she's just gone, she's gone – to remind myself that she's very much present in what she's given me makes me feel stronger. It makes me feel better.

L When you're thinking that she's gone, particularly at night, and you're feeling that sense of void, what do you tell yourself to feel stronger?

M What I'm going to tell myself is that she is still there with me. She didn't just raise me and give me those things. When I call upon her and think what would she do in a certain situation, right then, she's with me.

This is a palpable shift for Megan. To sense her mother as able to be called upon provides a balm to the sting of grief. She experiences the resource of relationship that has carried her in life and will continue to carry her. This is achieved by focusing on what remains, rather than on what is lost.

Lorraine Tell me about the shifts that are taking place from this conversation, Megan?

Megan It helps me… It's shifting me from, "She's just gone and you have to look at her photos and kind of remember her." and it's brought her more into the present with me on a daily basis, which I haven't thought of. I've only thought of her not being here and the loss that my kids aren't going to know her. Yeah, I thought I'd tell stories, but it was not the same. But I never thought about her shaping how I react in the present, or how I'm going to parent, or being with me when I crochet. It's honoring what she wanted. It's calming and reassuring. Gosh, I've been going through this pregnancy without her and it's like, "no, her love is there." In a way she's still there guiding me. She's still teaching me.

## Postscript

I asked Megan to read this account for accuracy and to add any comments about what reading it was like. We spoke after and she shared the following reflection of connecting with her mother's memory. Megan shared how her mother was "there" for her when she gardened, when she traveled, when she held her newborn daughter, or when she simply calmed her mind. "Sometimes I get frightened that she won't be there when I need her. I need to counter this with the love I have felt from her since she died. I had this sense of her telling me that she 'loved me enough for a thousand life times' when she was here, and this comforted me."

Megan, like many others in the face of grief, sustains herself through holding tight to the love and legacy that her mother created with her. It is this remembering practice that stands firmly against the stories of loss. And it is this practice that shapes a future, where the historical stories of the dead and the stories of the living are interwoven to craft an exquisite tapestry.

## References


Attig, T. (2001). Relearning the world: Making and finding meanings. In R. Neimeyer (Ed.), *Meaning reconstruction and the experience of loss* (pp. 33–54). Washington D.C.: American Psychological Association.

Belenky, M., Clinchy, B., Goldberger, N., & Tartule, J. (1986). *Women's way of knowing: The development of self, voice, and mind.* New York, NY: Basic Books.

Bowlby, J. (1969). *Attachment and loss* (Vol. 1). New York, NY: Basic Books.

Bowlby, J. (1973). *Attachment and loss* (Vol. 2). New York, NY: Basic Books.

Bruner, J. (1986). *Actual minds: Possible worlds.* Cambridge, MA: Harvard University Press.

Butler, J. (2004). *Precarious life: The powers of mourning and violence*. New York, NY: Verso.

Davies, B. (1991). The concept of agency: A feminist poststructuralist analysis. *Postmodern critical theorising, 30*, 42–53.
Deleuze, G. (1993). *The Fold: Leibniz and the Baroque*, (Tom Conley, Trans.) Minneapolis, MN: University of Minnesota Press.
Deleuze, G., & Parnet, C. (Eds.). (2002). The actual and the virtual. (E. R. Albert, Trans.). *Dialogues II* (pp. 148–152). New York, NY: Columbia University Press.
Freud, S. (1957). Mourning and melancholia. In J. Strachey (Ed. and Trans.). *The standard edition of the complete psychological works of Sigmund Freud* (Vol. 14, pp. 237–259). London, UK: Hogarth Press. (Original work published 1917).
Goldberger, N., Tartule, J., Clinchy, B., & Belenky, M. (1996). *Knowledge, difference, and power.* New York, NY: Basic Books.
Gergen, K. (1991). The saturated family. *Family Therapy Networker, 15*, 26–35.
Gergen, K. (2000). *The saturated self.* New York, NY: Basic Books.
Hagman, G. (2001). Beyond decathexis: toward a new psychoanalytic understanding and treatment of mourning. In R. Neimeyer (Ed.), *Meaning reconstruction and the experience of loss* (pp. 13–31). Washington, D.C: American Psychological Association.
Hare-Mustin, R. T., & Marecek, J. (1990). *Making a difference: Psychology and the construction of gender.* New Haven, CT: Yale University Press.
Hare-Mustin, R. (1991). The problem of gender in family therapy theory. In M. McGoldrick, C. Anderson, & F. Walsh (Eds.), *Women in families: A framework for family therapy* (pp. 61–77). New York, NY: Norton.
Hedtke, L. (2001). Dancing with death. *Gecko: A Journal of Deconstruction and Narrative Ideas in Therapeutic Practice, 2001*(2), 3–14.
Hedtke, L. (2012a). What's in an introduction? In R. Neimeyer (Ed.), *Techniques of grief therapy* (pp. 253–255). New York, NY: Routledge.
Hedtke, L. (2012b). *Breathing life into the stories of the dead: Constructing bereavement support groups.* Chagrin Falls, OH: Taos Institute Publications.
Hedtke, L. (2014). Creating stories of hope: A narrative approach to illness, death and grief. *Australian and New Zealand Journal of Family Therapy, 2014*(35), 4–19. doi:10.1002/anzf.1040
Hedtke, L., & Winslade, J. (2004). *Re-membering lives: Conversations with the dying and the bereaved.* Amityville, NY: Baywood.
Hedtke, L., & Winslade, J. (2005). The use of the subjunctive in re-membering conversations with those who are grieving. *Omega, 50*(3), 197–215. doi:10.2190/U1WC-WHA4-52GE-P2HH
Klass, D., Silverman, P., & Nickman, S. (Eds.). (1996). *Continuing bonds: New understandings of grief.* Philadelphia, PA: Taylor and Francis.
Kübler-Ross, E. (1969). *On death and dying.* New York, NY: Touchstone.
Lambert, R. (2002–2003). Constructing symbolic ancestry: Befriending time, confronting death. *Omega, 46*(4), 303–323. doi: 10.2190/EU0D-J1B0-JKJ0-GHMD
Lindemann, E. (1944). Symptomatology and management of acute grief. *American Journal of Psychiatry, 101*, 141–148.
McGoldrick, M. (2004). Gender and mourning. In F. Walsh & M. McGoldrick (Eds.), *Living beyond loss: Death in the family* (pp. 99–118). New York, NY: Norton.
Myerhoff, B. (1978). *Number our days.* New York, NY: Simon & Schuster.
Myerhoff, B. (1982). Life history among the elderly: Performance, visibility and remembering. In J. Ruby (Ed.), *A crack in the mirror: Reflexive perspectives in anthropology* (pp. 99–117). Philadelphia, PA: University of Pennsylvania Press.
Myerhoff, B. (2007). In M. Kaminsky & M. Weiss (Eds.), *Stories as equipment for living.* Ann Arbor, MI: The University of Michigan Press.
Nadeau, J. (1998). *Families making sense of death.* Thousand Oaks, CA: Sage.
Neimeyer, R. A. (2001). The language of loss: Grief therapy as a process of meaning reconstruction. In R. A. Neimeyer (Ed.), *Meaning reconstruction and the experience of loss* (pp. 261–292). Washington, DC: American Psychological Association.

Neimeyer, R. A., Klass, D., & Dennis, M. R. (2014). A social constructionist account of grief: Loss and the narration of meaning. *Death Studies, 38*, 485–498. doi:10.1080/07481187.2014.913454
Parkes, C. M. (1972). *Bereavement. Studies of grief in adult life*. New York, NY: International Universities Press.
Stroebe, M., & Schut, H. (2001). Meaning-making and the dual process model of coping with bereavement. In R. A. Neimeyer (Ed.), *Meaning reconstruction and the experience of loss* (pp. 55–73). Washington, DC: American Psychological Association.
Vickio, C. (1999). Together in spirit: Keeping our relationships alive when loved ones die. *Death Studies, 23*(2), 161–175. doi:10.1080/074811899201127
Walsh, F., & McGoldrick, M. (2004). Loss and the family: A systemic perspective. In F. Walsh & M. McGoldrick (Eds.), *Living beyond loss: Death in the family* (pp. 3–26). New York, NY: Norton.
Walsh, F., & Scheinkman, M. (1991). Models of family therapy. In M. McGoldrick, C. Anderson, & F. Walsh (Eds.), *Women in families: A framework for family therapy* (pp. 16–41). New York, NY: Norton.
Walter, T. (1999). *On bereavement: The culture of grief*. Buckingham, UK: Open University Press.
White, M. (1989). Saying hullo again. In M. White (Ed.), *Selected papers* (pp. 29–36). Adelaide, AU: Dulwich Centre Publications.
White, M. (2007). *Maps of narrative practice*. New York, NY: WW Norton.
Worden, J. W. (1991). *Grief counseling and grief therapy: A handbook for the mental health practitioner* (2nd ed.). New York, NY: Springer.
Worden, J. W. (2009). *Grief counseling and grief therapy: A handbook for the mental health practitioner* (4th ed.). New York, NY: Springer.

# Toward an Aesthetics of Engagement

**Colin James Sanders**

**Abstract** In this chapter, I describe some principle ideas informing and shaping of a therapeutic practice I refer to as aesthetics of engagement with struggling others. An aesthetics of engagement within the therapeutic context consists of multiple influences that continue to provide grounding and a framework for practice, yet a practice remaining open to additional inspirations. Accordingly, in this chapter, I describe philosophical, theological, and theoretical perspectives that have contributed toward this practice. The perspectives described in this chapter represent a synthesis of influences and inspirations that have evolved over many decades. As such, the tapestry informing an aesthetics of engagement is not intended to be at all prescriptive nor closed, as I believe it to remain a practice that continues to remain open to potential influences and encounters with the other, and to continue to evolve alongside news of difference (Bateson 1972).

## Toward an Aesthetics of Engagement

I take this use of the word 'spirit' to here refer to 'ethos'... White (2012, p. 168).

An aesthetics of engagement refers to the tapestry of relationships, influences, inspirations, and enchantments contributing to and comprising the ways in which

---

This chapter represents a much distilled and concise description and illustration of ideas, practices, and experiences discussed in the dissertation I wrote for my PhD, *Narrative poetics of resistance: Towards an aesthetics of engagement* (Sanders 2014).

C.J. Sanders (✉)
City University of Seattle, Vancouver, BC, Canada
e-mail: csanders@cityu.edu



V. Dickerson (ed.), *Poststructural and Narrative Thinking in Family Therapy*,
AFTA SpringerBriefs in Family Therapy, DOI 10.1007/978-3-319-31490-7_5

I approach therapeutic practice (Sanders 2014). As such, in practice, aesthetics of engagement[1] demonstrates a particular spirit, a particular ethical positioning, and a particular way of being human in relationship with others.

I consider myself fortunate in that I entered into this therapeutic profession initially as coordinator of an inner-city community school project involved with socioeconomically, often marginalized, children, and families, with a significant number of indigenous First Nations children. For me, the collaborative intention has always been about fomenting beneficial relationships, creating and building upon the presence within the relationship, listening and responding to co-identified needs and desires simply from a human, relational, perspective, opposed to a position unduly defined or directed by specific, totalizing, diagnostic criteria. From early on, the other for me was the person/family without equal access to education, social services, health and medical services, and meaningful employment. The other was the impoverished, invisible, person living "on the other side of the tracks."

In this chapter, I will highlight some theoretical influences informing my own practice, and throughout the points I am describing and discussing will be illustrated with memories and reflections derived from my lived experience in the field over these past forty years. I discuss the importance within therapeutic contexts of being hospitable, demonstrating presence, bearing witness, and attending to an expanded understanding of language. Additionally, I talk about my understanding and commitment to therapeutic engagement as representing both a sacred and a political act.

I have engaged with the thinking/writing of philosopher Emmanuel Levinas for many years and will briefly describe some aspects of his work that have appealed to, and inspired, my own work.[2]

## Emmanuel Levinas

A principle influence providing a framework for an aesthetics of engagement practice has been the thinking of philosopher Levinas (1987, 1993, 1995, 2001).[3]

Kapuscinski (2008), in a lecture on Levinas, observes, "…says Levinas, the Other has a face, and it is a sacred book in which good is recorded" (p. 35). Throughout my professional career, I count myself fortunate to have always had a profound belief and ethic that there exists goodness within all persons, regardless of

[1]For more thorough, practical illustrations of an aesthetics of engagement and a poetics of resistance in practice, see Sanders (1996, 1998, 2007, 2010, 2012, 2013), and Chapter Seven, Sanders (2014).

[2]For an intimate, personal, and historical appreciation of Levinas's contributions to philosophy and considerations of the other, see his friend Derrida (1999).

[3]Others, in their own fashion, have noted ways in which Levinas's thinking may be considered within therapeutic practice, education, and community development engagement (Chinnery and Bai 2008; Epston 2011; Larner 2004; Marmur 2002; Yukich and Hoskins 2011).

behaviors or actions they may have perpetrated. If I did not hold such a belief, I would not have been able to collaborate and work with many of the children (all under the age of 17) with whom I engaged between the years 1980 and 1986.

A couple of the young persons with whom I engaged were themselves responsible for the death of others, in violent circumstances, while others had perpetrated significant violations and injury toward others. Many of these young persons had also significantly inflicted injury upon themselves, through burning, razor blades, and knives. What I came to know of these young persons was that they all had themselves suffered horribly from the actions of others, more often than not from persons they were related to or knew well. I did not consider such experiences to excuse their own behaviors; I merely considered their experiences to be a factor within the context of their relationships toward others, and the environments within which they found themselves.

I have often thought, and said out loud in teaching contexts, that being involved in therapeutic collaboration requires commitment, patience, and compassion. This is a commitment to the facilitation of change, often involving change at the level of social policy, as well as a commitment to challenges of convention, tradition, and the normative and prescriptive taken-for-granted practices. Patience I would describe in terms of maintaining a presence that is not intent upon rushing in with needless words when silence abounds and being present as a silent witness will suffice. Compassion in terms of comprehending the suffering and struggle experienced or related by the other, while taking action at the same time to co-facilitate the removal of restraints and barriers the person, or persons, may be experiencing (Bateson 1972; White and Epston 1990).

Again, Levinas' thinking has been instructive and sustaining for me, in maintaining an ethic involving commitment, patience, and compassion. Levinas also provided an early critique to Western privileging of the individual over the relational, the collective, and the community, as described further below.

## Levinas and "Egology"

As imagined by Levinas, human beings are not the individualistic, materialistic, aspiring, competitive persons so familiar to North American psychology (Cushman 1995; Sampson 1991; White 2011), but are rather a person-for-others, first and foremost. Marmur (2002) writes, that along "With his teacher Edmund Husserl… the exponent of phenomenology, Levinas describes Western thought as 'egology'. His aim was to break out of this self-centered pattern in order to make room for the one the Bible calls 'your neighbor.' He wanted to move from dialectics to dialogue…" (pp. 5–6). In this sense, Levinas evolved what Breton (1995) referred to as a "…language of *relations*…" (p. 248), contributing early on to "…relational' thinking as [an] important corrective to the largely ego-centric perspective found in much contemporary psychology" (Freeman 2014, p. 1).

Levinas was committed to moving away from the ego-centered, individualistic, notion of human being long before considerations of relational thinking and relational being (Gergen 2009) appeared within contemporary therapeutic literature and therapeutic practice. This relational perspective on the co-creation of identity came to be a perspective shared by the co-founder of narrative therapy, White (2011), who wrote we need to "…underscore the phenomenon of a relational self rather than the phenomenon of the encapsulated self that is the vogue of contemporary Western culture" (p. 41).

I came to know "difference" and the other early on, when, as a child, my parents for a number of years took in international students attending the university where my father taught. Over the years, students from Africa, Sikh's from India, and French-speaking students from France lived with us and formed a part of our household. My parents were progressive, social democrats, and I recall as a young child election posters put up in our yard by the New Democratic Party (established 1961 in Canada) being defaced. My first girlfriend's parents were wary of me, even asking me if I was a Communist, because as a young teenager I participated in demonstrations for years against the US invasion of Vietnam and Cambodia. These early life experiences have, I believe, contributed to shaping my so-called professional life in particular ways.

I propose that practitioners interested in understanding the inter-relational significance and influences involved with the co-creation of human identity share more similarities than dissimilarities with Levinas. Buber's (1958) I/Thou relational thinking and dialogical philosophy also finds affinity with practitioners interested in relation being. In this context, McNamee and Hosking (2012) write,

> Both [Levinas and Buber] focus on the relational nature of human interchange. Levinas talks about ethics as a "first philosophy" from which knowledge emerges (a second philosophy), thereby reversing the philosophical trend that places knowledge as the first philosophy from which ethics emerge. *The idea that knowledge emerges from relational, ethical practice is wholly consistent with our argument here* [emphasis added]. Similarly, Buber features I-Thou relations over I-It relations, thereby acknowledging the central importance of relationality (p. 98).

Levinas's thinking regarding the other offers an important contribution to the therapeutic literature associated with the turn toward dialogue and the dialogical. The therapeutic implications of a distinctly dialogical philosophy have influenced many practitioners adhering to social constructionist, collaborative, narrative, and poststructuralist influenced therapeutic practices (Anderson 2007a, b, 2012; Anderson and Goolishian 1988; Andersen 1995, 1996, 2007, 2012; Larner 2004; Lock and Strong 2010; Sanders 2014; Shotter 2015; Seikula 2002, 2011; Seikkula and Trimble 2005), and no doubt we will witness further developments highlighting dialogical, discursive theory and practice in the coming years.[4]

Levinas proposes a way of being present with others, greeting and attending to, and being welcoming and hospitable toward the other. Levinas further proposes an

[4]See Strong and Pare (2004).

ethic of hospitality in recognition of the stranger; this hospitable presence situates the practitioner as host to the other, or, others. Levinas's thinking invites implications for social policy in welcoming the immigrant, newcomer, asylum seeker, and the refugee, and facilitating the sociocultural inclusion of newcomers.[5]

Levinas initiates and creates an aesthetics of engagement with the other that is profoundly relational; an aesthetics of engagement conceptualizing our understanding of self or identity as being but a concatenation[6] of our lived, social, relational, experience with all others with whom we have been in relationship, been informed by, inspired by, or struggled along with toward mutual understanding(s).

Finally, Levinas, building upon Buber (1958), proposes dialogue as a bridge toward transcending intransigence, difference, and opposition; dialogue as a way toward dissolving and resolving human dilemmas (Anderson and Goolishian 1988) and problems of everyday living. As such, Levinas's thinking has much to offer practitioners within an aesthetics of engagement and other therapeutic practices.

In the following section, I will discuss the practice of an aesthetics of engagement viewed as a "human art" (Andersen 2012), a non-pathologizing practice and art, and a practice attentive to and attuned to the cultural and ideological discourses and influences embedded within any therapeutic context (Foucault 1980; White 1991, 1997). Attending to collaborative therapeutic engagement with others has always seemed to me to be more about craft than technique, and considering these practices to be a form of human art has strengthened and encouraged me.

## Therapeutic Practice as Human Art

I have long imagined that engaging within therapeutic, conversational practices was a performance and commitment involving craft, a craft and an art significantly informed by inter-relationship and less so by technique and intervention. I have also long considered therapeutic engagement to represent a political act, insofar as the therapist assumes an ethical position in terms of viewing psychological dilemmas as arising within sociocultural contexts (Martin-Baro 1994; White and Epston 1990).

Having worked within domains of counseling, community development, and counselor education over forty years, all too often I have encountered practitioners and systems lacking in compassion, justice, and civility due to dogmatism, an attraction to diagnoses, and an interpersonal discomfort in being with others who are different. I have heard practitioners describe persons as, "my anorectics," and "she's just a borderline," "what do you expect, he's an addict," and other such demeaning, denigrating, and totalizing language. I have collaborated with many

[5]Given the current concern with the reactionary response by some towards accepting and settling such persons around the world, we would do well to be instructed and guided by Levinas's philosophy of the other.

[6]Here, I wish to acknowledge Tomm's (1993) observation that "I regard a personal story as a concatenation of internalized conversation…" (p. 75).

persons over the years who have entered into therapy under the impression that they themselves *are* the problem and that they themselves are responsible for being the problem, having no comprehension of the sociocultural, socioeconomic, multifactorial material conditions may lead to distress or despair.

Many masters of counseling graduate students I have collaborated with over the years have also expressed to me profound relief having been exposed to the narrative therapy practice of externalizing problems, or removing the problem from the person and arriving at an understanding of the very multiple social, cultural, engendered, and other factors involved in the creation of the problem identity (Sanders 2012).

As my thinking evolved regarding therapeutic practice perceived as aesthetics of engagement, Andersen's (2012) proposal of therapeutic work as a human art benefitted me and strengthened my perspective. Andersen wrote, "My wish is at the moment we stop talking about therapy and research as human techniques, and rather talk of it as human art; the art to participate in the bonds with others. If we exclusively started to use the word 'human art' how would that bewitch our understanding and our lives?" (p. 52).

Such a way of engaging within practice as a human art also evoked Anderson and Goolishian's (1988) orientation toward a therapeutic engagement of awaiting the *un-said*, and a patient, abiding, practice of awaiting the *not-yet-said*, inherent within a larger *not-knowing* philosophical position.

Again, early on in my own collaboration with young persons struggling with substance use (Sanders 1996, 1998) and with adults (Sanders 2007), listening for the not-yet-said formed an important component in terms of engaging with others. Specifically, keeping my own thoughts in abeyance, leaving space for the other to think out loud, to speak their mind and their heart, became more meaningful than filling in space out of discomfort with silence.

A not-knowing ethical position allowed me to be open to a particular vulnerability, a vulnerability inviting of inquiry, curiosity, and human belonging, myself with another. Below, I further discuss such vulnerability in terms of presence. Such an ethical position allows for a compassionate attending to, and engagement with, others within a context of hospitality. Taking such a perspective also invites an entry point into the mystery and adventure of experiencing whom the other may be, or may be becoming, relationally within conversation with a practitioner of the human art.[7]

I believe that proceeding from this philosophical position in practice benefits the persons with whom we collaborate in a number of ways. Persons who consult with us who are struggling with a variety of dilemmas, or persons who are suffering for a variety of reasons, come to realize that there is nothing specific nor particular required of them; there are no correct responses necessary, and there exists space, in such an aesthetics of engagement, for imagination, for wonder, for inquiry, reflection and questioning. Many persons experience this as being extremely

[7]For an intriguing, enlightening perspective on the mystery of the other, see Freeman (2014).

different from the professional, expert advice they have often encountered and been recruited into.

My practice has been inspired by thinking of an aesthetics of engagement more as a poetic and sacred way of approaching how we might engage with struggling others. Again, I have been influenced by forebears who have conceived of their own practice in more philosophical, than theory based, ways. For example, Anderson (2007) has written that it is her intention is to "…distinguish my work as a 'philosophy of life' in action, as an approach and not as a theory or model of therapy" (p. 43). White (1997), when asked to describe how he himself perceived of his way of engaging with others, reflected, "Well, as I wouldn't define it as an approach, it is hard for me to really talk limitations in the usual way. Is this work better defined as a world-view? Perhaps, but even then this is not enough. Perhaps it is an epistemology, a philosophy, a personal commitment, a politics, an ethics, a practice, a life and so on…" (p. 37). Regarding the sacred, I share with New Zealand's The Family Centre, a belief that "sacredness…refers to the deepest respect for humanity, its qualities and the environment" (Waldegrave et al. 2003, p. 75) and that this view of the sacred is one "more akin to the sacredness of life or 'soul' as in soul music" (p. 75).

What all these practitioners of the human art of therapeutic engagement share is an abhorrence of therapeutic violence (Freedman and Combs 1996) and a resistance to evaluation, diagnostic assessment, and any judgment in regard to the efforts and resourcefulness of struggling others. A practice conceptualized as an aesthetics of engagement shares in such a rejection.

One way to avoid the all-too-easy tendency to blame others for their suffering and struggles, to pathologize and denigrate, is to engage with others bearing in mind some of the ideas and concepts described within this chapter. The practice of the human art of therapy cannot be distilled down to a repertoire of techniques, strategies, and interventions; rather, the craft and art of therapeutic conversation represents a dialogical engagement, an encounter involving considerations of presence, and careful attention to the words being used in describing struggles arising within the increasing array of problems and dilemmas encountered in the act of day to day living.

An aesthetics of engagement thus represents a practice in direct distinction to the increasing tendency to medicalize, psychologize, or neurologize interpersonal tensions, dissension, struggles, and dilemmas. White (2011) discussed what he referred to as "the psychologization of life" referring to ways in which so-called, constructed, theoretical ideas and professional knowledge manufactured and supported the psychologization of life in a social environment that Szasz (2007) critiqued as representing the "therapeutic state." White wrote, "This psychologization of life is achieved through a network of universal truth claims that obscures the extent to which professional knowledge are culture-specific and the extent to which they are manufactured through specific historical and political processes" (p. 66). Any consideration of how so-called psychological dilemmas take shape and arise must also take into consideration the social, cultural, and ideological matrix involved. Not to take such domains into consideration leads advertently, or inadvertently, toward the pathologizing of persons (Tomm 1990, 1991).

I next address a philosophical practice that is hospitable and inviting of dialogue, one that engages within the mystery of the other (Levinas 1987, 2001).

## The Mystery of the Other

Levinas (2001) suggests the other can never completely be known nor comprehended. Levinas reflects upon the mystery of the other, and the often mysterious inter-relationship within which self and other are always engaged, "The relationship with the other is not an idyllic and harmonious relationship of communion, or a sympathy through which we put ourselves in the other's place; we recognize the other as resembling us, but exterior to us; the relationship with the other is a relationship with a Mystery" (1987, p. 75).

In a context of therapeutic engagement, the craft of contending patiently with ambiguity, and at times coexisting and being with silences, appears to be an imperative requirement, if the other is to be acknowledged and respected. Ambiguity and uncertainty may invite further inquiry, the asking of intentional questions, for example, the purpose of which is to become informed and enlightened by the other in regard to the words they use to articulate their experience as well as the particular and specific meaning(s) they ascribe to the words. Navigating such a liminal space, being both accepting of and patient with uncertainty, proceeding tentatively, awaiting the unexpected and the not-yet-said, represents a particular way of encountering and bearing witness to the words and being of the other.

I have always been of the belief that as human beings we are always only beginning to arrive upon the shores of an understanding of the other; becoming a part of, and connected to, a sense of the presence of the other, whether an intimate partner, child, grandchild, friend, acquaintance, colleague, student, neighbor. Our knowing of the other must always be approximate, tentative, as the other's identity, as is our own, will always be shifting, ebbing and flowing, transforming, in flux. Early on in practice, I came to realize the only way I would come to "know" of the other would be through relationship, not through a reading of a so-called psychological report or clinical file (Harre 1984).

If it becomes accepted and acknowledged there will always be something of the ineffable, the poetic, in regard to coming to know and understand the other, then one need allow space for contemplating the nuances, intricacies, and mysteries that comprise persons, and also contribute to the richly textured depth and soul of the other, with whom we enter into community and communion, continually defining, re-defining, and refining our ways of coexisting, and going on together (Wittgenstein 2009).

Entering into an encounter with the mystery of the other requires that therapists be not only engaged in particular ways, but that they also be open to the experience of the other in ways that invite vulnerability. I envisage such vulnerability as a form of bearing witness to the words and emotions of the other; at times, such bearing witness will involve a response in words, and, at other times, a silent witnessing may be all that is required by way of responding to the other. I believe there are some stories that one cannot respond in words to, but as practitioners of the human art of therapeutic engagement, we can let the other become aware of our acknowledgment of their stories by simply, gracefully, being present in the moment with them.

## Bearing Witness and the Sacred

Previously, I have described elements comprising a notion of the sacred that I relate to in therapeutic work. I consider this notion of the sacred to form an integral, ethical groundwork upon which an aesthetics of engagement proceeds (Sanders 2013, 2014). Gergen (1998) once proposed an "expanded dialogue" on constructive therapeutic ideas and practices that had hitherto become marginalized or subjugated within the domain of therapeutic practice, proposing, "This expanded dialogue should also include voices otherwise marginalized by the therapeutic establishment. I think here especially of the teeming number of therapists whose practices are nourished by the discourse of spirit, love, and God, and yet who are unable to gain legitimacy in speaking of these matters. These therapists represent rich and significant traditions within the culture" (p. xx).

Comprehending the therapeutic encounter as a sacred act (and political act, as discussed below) invites the therapist into a particular form of conversation, of dialogue, with suffering others. I would suggest this form of dialogue is marked by a deeply acknowledged and sincerely pronounced respect for and honoring of the person(s) who are consulting, regardless of behaviors they may have engaged in. To engage in this respect does not mean the specifics of the behaviors are ignored; rather, persons become "invited" to begin to be accountable and accept responsibility for acts they have perpetrated that have injured, violated, or oppressed others (Jenkins 1990).

Of course, there exist multiple ways in which we may go on together, and utilizing language and dialogue is one of the more predominant ways. The purpose and intention of such dialogue within the sacred encounter with the other is to arrive at mutual understandings and comprehensions of disparate beliefs and knowledge, without being recruited into violence or violation.

There are multiple ways of experiencing and engaging within such conversations. Buber (1965), in a conversation with the humanistic psychologist Carl Rogers, remarked, "…what interests me more than anything: human effective dialogue. Meaning by dialogue not just talking. Dialogue can be silence… We could sit together, or rather walk together in silence, and that would be a dialogue" (p. 175).[8]

---

[8]Here, I am reminded in Buber's passage of the contemplative reflections collected in Thomas Merton's (2001) *Dialogues with Silence*.

How is it that silence can be dialogue? I believe this question can be answered by a discussion of what it means to be present, and to have presence, in the company of another person, or persons.

Some years ago, I was consulted by a woman, "Margaret[9]," in her sixties, whose husband had recently died. Margaret had been married to her husband only ten years, having met, as she said, "late in their lives" through mutual friends. Her husband was twenty years her senior. She informed me that they had known when first they decided to live together there existed a possibility of his dying before her. Furthermore, Margaret informed me she had been somewhat prepared for his death, but "one is never fully prepared." I agreed with Margaret that one is never fully prepared and asked her what would be most beneficial for her in terms of our meeting. Margaret reflected, saying, "I really think what might be most beneficial for me would be for you to simply listen to me, listen to how I am thinking now of the ten years John and I had together, ten wonderful years, your listening to me would be most beneficial."

Margaret had been told by friends and her employer that she "should talk to someone" following the death of her companion. A couple of her friends had told her that she may be "suffering from the loss of John" and should look into "grief counseling." Margaret had decided that what she needed was quite simple: a person to listen to her quiet, at times tearful, recollection, and celebration of the wonderful years she had spent together with John.

Margaret informed me of the traveling she had John had shared, the galleries visited, and the paintings and sculptures they saw. Margaret told me of their walks along the river, summer and winter, and the simplicity and non-materialism of the life they shared in. One question I did ask directly of her was, "What would John have wished and hoped for you in the event he died before you did?" To this question, Margaret responded quietly and thoughtfully, recalling John's encouragement for her to find ways to continue on after his death, and especially his hope she would be sustained in her life by the memories of their time together.

Margaret returned three weeks later to inform me she was getting out of the house more, had commenced reconnecting with friends, with whom she attended an opera, was also going to yoga and had started painting again. Margaret said, in effect, she was getting on with her life, "as John would have wanted me to."

It is with such an understanding in mind that I purposefully and intentionally imagine and create the space and domain in which an aesthetics of engagement occurs, when bearing witness to the struggles and the stories of others within therapeutic conversation.[10]

---

[9]"Margaret" is a pseudo-name.

[10]White's (1997) concept of "remembering practices," building upon Myerhoff's (1982) "re-membering" practices, has often been useful in conceptualizing this form of engagement; for a more detailed description of the application of such a concept, see Hedke's chapter in this book.

## Becoming Hospitable

There is a sense in which therapy has always been understood as involving hospitality, that is to say, as a particular way of welcoming suffering, struggling others into a domain in which purposeful and transformative conversation may occur. In the spirit of hospitality, I have written elsewhere of "welcoming ceremonies" and related practices in my work at the Vancouver, Canada Peak House, a live-in program for young persons struggling with substance use (Sanders 2014). Many of our practices were inspired by indigenous, ritual and ceremonial, practices of "belonging" (Waldegrave et al. 2003), learned through our connection with the indigenous persons collaborating with us at Peak House, or, visiting with us as cultural consultants (Sanders 1996, 1998, 2007; Waldegrave et al. 2003).

Such a philosophy of being hospitable has become more pronounced and highlighted within the collaborative and discursive therapeutic perspectives. Anderson (2012), for example, writes "Hospitality involves subtleties and nuances of greetings and meetings that shape the tone and quality of the relationship and conversation, and consequently their potential… The therapist is both a temporary host and guest in the client's life" (p. 15).

Such an invitation and invocation for the therapist to be hospitable harkens back to the philosophy of Levinas.

> Should language be thought uniquely as the communication of an idea or as information, and not also – and perhaps above all – as the fact of encountering the other as other, that is to say, already as response to him? [sic] Is not the first word *bonjour*. *Bonjour* as benediction and my being available for the other man [sic] (2001, p. 47).

"*Bonjour* as benediction"—or a greeting in any language—I find to be a poetic invitation resonating an *ethos,* a spirit of comfort, a gesture of putting the other at ease, of inviting the other to sit in peace around the metaphorical hearth and fire, or, the common table where food and wine are shared, and discover convergences and affinities, amid apparent differences. At Peak House, for example, we came to discover and appreciate the importance of welcoming the other into the community in a ceremonial way, in terms of inviting a belonging to the Peak House community (Sanders 2014; Waldegrave et al. 2003).

As therapists and practitioners engaging within Andersen's (2012) human art, we are invited into the therapeutic relationship, never knowing for just how long such a relationship may persist. Perhaps, in one sense, it may be useful to consider each therapeutic encounter as being possibly both the first and the last encounter, as some practitioners of brief therapies have suggested.

Within a therapeutic practice, when encountering a person, or persons, struggling with a particular dilemma, it would seem that being hospitable and welcoming is the initial ethical position required for such an experience. Some observers of so-called master therapists consider that what therapists do, in fact, is representative of common sense (Lomas 1999).

Offering and creating a hospitable context or environment in which to converse, share intimate stories (Waldegrave et al. 2003), seek resolution of differences, mutual understanding, peaceful accord, and so on also requires a particular ethic of presence on behalf of the therapist or practitioner.

## Presence Within an Aesthetics of Engagement

There exists an abundance of research, based upon client feedback, pointing out a crucial correlation between the presence of the therapist and person within the therapeutic relationship in regard to factors facilitating change and transformation (Duncan et al. 2010).

Earlier relational traditions also speak to a particular way of being with others, and particular understandings of what being present entails. For example, in a discussion of the I/Thou philosophy of Martin Buber, Scott (2014) discusses a particular sense of having *presence* and a way to experience and be with "holy insecurity" (pp. 330–332) observing, "'Becoming a self' is a relational process, but the corollary is also true: bringing a full presence to the engagement contributes to it becoming a dialogue" (p. 330).

Again, entering into the mystery of the other, being in communion with the other, arriving at co-created, new meanings, new understandings, seems to represent one of the primary focuses when anyone is engaging in therapeutic conversation. Engaging with others in this sense of presence may entail an experience that goes where words and language may not go.

Bird (1994) suggests that we may benefit from being with others in connection, as "Connection provides us with an enquiry resource beyond the language used by people to represent experience. Connection assists us to listen for intonation, emotions, body sensations, visions, dreams, the imagination, and for what is partially said" (p. 93). Such a way of re-thinking the boundaries of language fits within an aesthetics of engagement, offering, as it does, an expanded understanding of human experience, an experience moving beyond language.

Within the context of such experience and engagement, acceptance of the other becomes entwined within presence, demonstrating a nonjudgmental, non-evaluative, way of encountering and engaging with the other; acceptance, not assessment; presence, not prescription. In therapeutic conversation, acceptance and presence contribute to the co-creation of meaning, or, new meaning(s), within a linguistic field, a field that is not neutral. I believe it is not neutral, because I believe that the intention and purpose within such conversation is to understand the restraints or the barriers operating for a person or persons, within a context of relationship (with others, with their environment, with organizations and systems of one sort or another) that impede their going on. As such, aesthetics of engagement represents an intentional, purposeful, focused, collaboration, or adventure.

Regardless of the theoretical perspective(s) informing one's practice, there exists common ground in the belief that, for the person(s) seeking a therapeutic consultation, the relationship between the person and therapist is most important in ushering in hope for transformation, change, and difference, while the theoretical perspective(s) employed are of less importance (Duncan et al. 2010). Again, we are speaking here of a relational way of being, a relational way of proceeding.

Such a manner of being with others, in community and in communion (Byrne in McCarthy 2004), invites a particular understanding of, and engagement with, the politics of experience (Laing 1967).

## Language and the Politics of Experience

Language is love (Blaser 2008, p. 506).

Maturana and Varela propose, "…the biological foundation of social phenomena is love" (1987, p. 246). Through language, through love, we come to a recognition and celebration of the extraordinary mystery comprising the multiplicity of ways by which human beings make meaning and share meaning(s). What holds meaning for us comprises just what we have agreed is meaningful; who we are is formed and informed within the shared meanings of such inter-relationships, which we refer to as community. The web of kinship only makes sense and is meaningful if we believe there is meaning to be made, relationally between us. Language shapes experience and assists in the articulation of experience. That said, we are also aware of the way in which language falls short or struggles with articulating the ineffable, the mystery, and the wonder of relationship and of human being, and of being human (Andersen 2007; Freeman 2014; Shotter 2015).

Irish writer, Samuel Beckett (1975), has a character reflect at the end of his novel, *The Unnamable*, uttering, "You must go on. I can't go on. I'll go on" (p. 132). And, to reiterate, more often than not, in an aesthetics of engagement, we go on through and with language, invoking dialogue, not digression, estrangement, alienation, and isolation. So, how is we manifest the will to go on, to continue to hope, to continue to be, in the face of adversity, anguish, despair, exploitation, oppression? In therapeutic contexts, I believe one such way is through the presence of the practitioner, as demonstrated in a particular way.

Andersen (2012), commenting upon a video of White conversing with a couple, observed, "If somebody should ask me what Michael does, what is his practice, I would highlight his strong, warm *presence* [emphasis added]. What I also noticed was that sometimes, I think even several times they said something and they came up with a concept, he said, 'What does it mean?' He is very active in finding the meaning of the words" (p. 154). Gergen (2009) observed, "Narrative therapy is outstanding in its sensitivity to the way in which meaning is molded in relationship. Therapists understand that life narratives are born within relationships, and that such relationships may be lodged within institutions and the mass media" (p. 300).

Andersen (2007) always appeared to be especially attentive to the components of a relational language as utilized by those with whom he collaborated, insisting language needs to be understood in a particular, contextual way. I believe that Andersen's expanded description of the human activity that constitutes language is important to be aware of in any discussion regarding dialogical therapeutic practice:

> Language is here defined as all expressions, which are regarded to be of great significance in the mentioned communal perspective. They are of many kinds, for instance to talk, write, paint, dance, sing, point, cry, laugh, scream, hit etc., are all bodily activities. When these expressions, which are bodily, take place in the presence of others, language becomes a social activity. Our expressions are social offerings for participating in the bonds with others (p. 88).

Language is not merely words, and just exactly what words mean and connote shift and change over time and within particular contexts, as Wittgenstein (2009) and others have pointed out (Bateson 1979).

The Dalai Lama once commented that being compassionate is not enough, one must also act. I believe that all therapeutic practices occur within a sociopolitical context (Foucault 2006). White (2012), when asked if his interviewing practice might be "a dialogical practice," responds making the following important point, "It is dialogical, but anything dialogical is also cultural and historical" (p. 147), and these cultural and historical influences and discourses need be considered in how psychological dilemmas become created, constructed, and deconstructed.

Ideology is not inseparable from an understanding of any perspective describing a therapeutic practice (Alexander and Shelton 2014; Cushman 1995; Foucault 1980). Relational collaboration of any sort involves relations of power (Foucault 1980; Hare-Mustin 1994). All our relationships are imbued within and shaped within politics, as the feminist adage of the 60s insisted, "the personal is political." White (2011) wrote, "…therapy has played a cardinal role in the reproduction and production of dominant culture" and

> [Therapy] has been a major player in the maintenance of the dominant social order. It has made an entirely significant contribution to the valorization of certain ways of life and to the marginalization of other ways of life. In regard to the hegemony of the lionized knowledges of this culture, psychotherapy has been duplicit (p. 52).

McNamee (2015) shares the concern that therapeutic practice has often been complicit in insisting that psychological dilemmas and struggles are the fault of the individual; as McCarthy (1995) puts it, such dilemmas and struggles are perceived as being individual problems, not social problems. McNamee (2015) proposes a therapeutic practice invoking the radical presence of relational being, inviting us into positioning our therapeutic practice in such a way that we become more open to comprehending the complexity of the communities within which we abide, and more present in our appreciation for the differences existing amongst us (p. 381).

Living together, coexisting and co-creating, would appear to be what being human entails, yet, as we are painfully aware, there also exists extreme adversity, animosity, political terror and torture, and racist reaction and prejudice within the global context. Accordingly, the following section will briefly discuss the global consideration of immigrant other, in the context of aesthetics of engagement, and ways in which such a perspective may offer hope for newcomers to new countries.

## The Immigrant Other, the Homeless, and Being Hospitable

> The Other is, for example, the weak, the poor, "the widow and the orphan," whereas I am the rich or the powerful (Levinas 1987, p. 83).

Robinson (1990), in her inaugural address as the first woman to become President of Ireland, invoked the ancient Celtic metaphor of the Fifth Province, speaking to how the other, in this instance immigrants from countries other than Ireland, might become welcomed and received in a hospitable manner. The metaphor of the Irish Fifth Province refers to a Druidic domain in which warring clans and tribes could enter without weapons, for the purpose of conversation and dialogue directed at peaceful resolution of outstanding differences and resentments; this metaphor has long been an important consideration within the therapeutic practice of Byrne and McCarthy (1998, 2007) and McCarthy (1995, 2000, 2004, 2010).

Over the years, I have often invoked the Fifth Province metaphor in practice, explaining the concept to the persons consulting with me, or to group participants I have been involved with, in order to intentionally create and offer up an environment in which disagreement and dissent can be talked about, with the purpose of re-solution and re-conciliation in mind.

More recently, Pope Francis, in New York at the United Nations, spoke of the ethical imperative of welcoming the other, refugees, and asylum seekers, among us. These days especially, the "other" figures are in the global news, as walls, both literal and metaphorical, are being constructed to keep others from becoming welcomed, supported, and otherwise assisted by social services.

Coming toward the end of this chapter, I wish to move from the micro-level of therapeutic engagement, to a more global consideration as regards suffering, struggling others. In her poem "Spirit of Place" (1980), Adrienne Rich wrote that "Strangers are an endangered species," and these days we increasingly hear of, and witness, the effects of a lack of hospitality, the lack of compassion, and the lack of understanding visited upon so many.

As I write this chapter, thousands of persons are departing their countries of origin, in search of hospitality in other countries new to them. Sadly however, newcomers, refugees, and persons seeking asylum from political strife and/or religious oppression are also eliciting xenophobic and racist reactions. Regarding the other, whether a person encountered in a therapeutic context or arriving as a newcomer to another country, an aesthetics of engagement calls for hospitable practices of social inclusivity (Marmur 2002), and a political commitment to fund social programs to assist struggling others in sustainable ways.

Marmur invokes Levinas's "ethical reflections on social inclusion" in addressing the need for just such a political commitment from government to address systemic inequalities and unequal access to resources, including employment, health care, and education. Marmur proposes, "Social inclusion reflects a proactive, human development approach to social wellbeing that calls for more than the removal of barriers or risks. It requires investments and action to bring about the conditions for inclusion, as the population health and international human development movements have taught us" (p. viii).

In the context of assisting newcomers, political and religious refugees, and asylum seekers arriving in some Canadian cities, DeFehr et al. (2012) have described the spirit of their collaborative and dialogical practice in terms influenced by Anderson and Goolishian's (1988) not-knowing philosophical perspective, and Levinas's ethics regarding a socially just engagement with the other. It is encouraging to learn of such practices, as I think the implications of this work offer hope for struggling others, in ways that maintain human dignity and honor the resourcefulness of persons forced to seek refuge. I am not suggesting this is the only way to proceed within an engagement with the immigrant other, merely that this is one perspective that resonates and is meaningful for me when considering some of the ideas and concepts discussed within this chapter.

In 2010, I was the lead on a national research demonstration project,[11] known as the At Home/*Chez Soi* research project, based upon a "housing first" model, in which participants in the low barrier project were provided with housing first, without being required to first go to detox, treatment, or become involved in any other social service, or mandated group context. The project I was involved with was comprised of a transdisciplinary team available 24/7 to participants, in recognition of our awareness that problems do not keep office hours nor recognize holidays (Sanders 2010).

Engaging with participants within this project really brought home to me the practical applicability of the philosophical notion of being hospitable, of being welcoming toward struggling, suffering, others. In a weekly group, named by participants as the "Becoming an Insider" group (i.e., moving from being street homeless to moving inside into one's own apartment) participants would be welcome to share their stories and partake in a meal with one another. Participants were asked only to be nonviolent, both in the language they employed with one another,

[11]The project, known as At Home/*Chez Soi* took place in five Canadian cities, over a period of four years. For 14 months, I was the lead on the assertive community treatment (ACT) team, with Rain City Housing First, Vancouver, British Columbia (Sanders 2010). We provided supportive housing to persons who had been chronically homeless, were engaged with substance use, and had a *DSM* diagnosis (the criterion for participants in the Vancouver research). (*Mental Health Commission of Canada, Vancouver Final Report: At Home/Chez Soi Project*, 2014).

and in their physical presence. There was no guideline excluding participants who were arriving at group under the influence of substances, only a guideline that substances could not be used on site.[12]

In the collaborations, I have embarked upon with struggling, suffering others, the relationship between the other and myself has always remained integral, framed and understood within the context of ideas, concepts, and philosophies briefly described here. I believe a certain amount of influence regarding my aesthetics of engagement derived from my own early childhood, familial, experiences, co-evolving alongside my reading among various disciplines. This wide array of reading led me to continually consider ways to integrate and apply multiple ideas in an ethically coherent, meaningful, beneficial way. Arriving at the end of my chapter here, I would hasten, to say, further adventures along these lines are imminent.

## Summary

As therapists and practitioners, we co-evolve and facilitate, as architects of dialogue, the going on, one with an-other, within an aesthetics of engagement. I have briefly described aesthetics of engagement as being a practice demonstrating and performing of presence, acceptance, witnessing, hospitality, and an adherence toward the ethical position of therapeutic love, a practice in opposition and resistance to therapeutic violence. Such a practice stands in distinction to practices that would pathologize and objectify persons, or in any way violate the other. An aesthetics of engagement is focused upon punctuating and highlighting strengths, abilities, resourcefulness, knowledge, and the wisdom of struggling, suffering others.

In this chapter, I have briefly introduced and described particular philosophical, theological ideas and concepts, in addition to a critique of normative and prescriptive psychological perspectives informing and shaping of an aesthetics of engagement. To reiterate, this practice cannot be interpreted or performed in an orthodox manner, and this practice remains an open field, a domain open to further conversation, influences, and inspirations.

I have also described such an engagement as being simultaneously sacred and political. I have discussed principle ideas comprising this practice within the context of a socially inclusive, socially just, practice and aesthetic of engagement with struggling others. I have discussed the mystery and the privilege of coexisting with others within therapeutic contexts and moved briefly to some thoughts on welcoming immigrant others as newcomers, and regarding hospitality within the context of collaborating with homeless persons.

---

[12]The "Becoming an Insider" groups were creatively co-facilitated by Baumgarten and Williams (2014) and Williams and Baumgarten (2014).

Writing of Levinas, Kapuscinski (2008) cites Barbara Skarga, noting that "...his philosophy is a framework that you have to fill in with your own experience and observations" (p. 36). Accordingly, in this chapter, I have provided some context for the above-mentioned ideas, concepts, and perspectives in terms of my own work experience in a variety of practices over the past four decades. For me, the points described above do not exist as metaphysical ideas separated from practical use; these points can be actualized and have practical applications within therapeutic, educational, organizational, and community work contexts. As such, I remain grateful to those others with whom I have engaged over the decades, recalling Buber's (1958) words that "In the beginning is relation" (p. 18), and Rimbaud's, "I is another."

## References

Alexander, B. K., & Shelton, C. P. (2014). *A history of psychology in western civilization*. Cambridge UK: Cambridge University Press.
Andersen, T. (1995). Reflecting processes; acts of informing and forming. You can borrow my eyes but you must not take them away from me! In S. Friedman (Ed.), *The reflecting team in action: Collaborative practice in family therapy*. New York & London: Guilford.
Andersen, T. (1996). Language is not innocent. In F. W. Kaslow (Ed.), *Handbook of relational diagnosis and dysfunctional family patterns* (pp. 119–125). New York, NY: Wiley.
Andersen, T. (2007). Human participation: Human "Being" is the step for human "Becoming" in the next step. In H. Anderson & G. Gehart (Eds.), *Collaborative therapy: Relationships and conversations that make a difference*. New York, NY: Routledge.
Andersen, T. (2012). Words—Universes travelling by. In T. Malinen, S. J. Cooper & F. N. Thomas (Eds.), *Masters of narrative and collaborative therapies: The voices of Andersen, Anderson, and White*. New York & London: Routledge.
Anderson, H. (2007a). A postmodern umbrella: Language and knowledge as relational and generative, and inherently transforming. In H. Anderson & D. Gehart (Eds.), *Collaborative therapy: Relationships and conversations that make a difference* (pp. 7–19). New York, NY: Routledge.
Anderson, H. (2007b). The heart and spirit of collaborative therapy: The philosophical stance—"A way of being" in relationship and conversation. In H. Anderson & D. Gehart (Eds.), *Collaborative therapy: Relationships and conversations that make a difference* (pp. 43–59). New York, NY: Routledge.
Anderson, H. (2012). Collaborative relationships and dialogic conversations: Ideas for a relationally responsive practice. *Family Process, 51*(1), 8–24.
Anderson, H, & Goolishian, H. A. (1988). Human systems as linguistic systems: Preliminary and evolving ideas about the implications for clinical theory. *Family Process*, 27(4), 371–395.
Bateson, G. (1972). *Steps to an ecology of mind*. New York, NY: Ballantine books.
Bateson, G. (1979). *Mind and nature: A necessary unity*. New York, NY: Bantam Books.
Baumgartner, B., & Williams, B. (2014). Becoming and insider: Narrative therapy groups alongside people overcoming homelessness. *Journal of Systemic Therapies, 33*(4), 1–14.
Beckett, S. (1975). *The Unnamable*. London, UK: Calder & Boyars.
Bird, J. (1994). *The heart's narrative: Therapy and navigating life's contradictions*. Auckland, NZ: Edge Press.
Blaser, R. (2008). *The holy forest*. Berkeley, CA: University of California Press.

Breton, S. (1995). Being, god and the poetics of relation. In R. Kearney (Ed.), *States of mind: Dialogues with contemporary thinkers*. Washington Square, NY: New York University Press.
Buber, M. (1958). *I and thou*. (2nd edn, R. G. Smith Trans.). New York, NY: Charles Scribner's & Sons.
Buber, M. (1965). *The knowledge of man: A philosophy of the interhuman*. (M.S. Friedman, & R. G. Smith Trans.). New York, NY: Harper & Row.
Byrne, N., & McCarthy, I. (1998). Marginal illuminations. In M. McGoldrick (Ed.), *Re-visioning family therapy*. Guilford: New York, NY.
Byrne, N., & McCarthy, I. (2007). The dialectical structure of hope and despair: A fifth province approach. In C. Flaskas, I. McCarthy, & J. Sheehan (Eds.), *Hope and despair in narrative and family therapy: Reflections on adversity, forgiveness and reconciliation*. Hove and New York: Brunner/Routledge.
Chinnery, A. & Bai, H. (2008). Levinas and responsibility. In D. Egea-Kuehn (Ed.), *Levinas and education*. London: Routledge.
Cushman, P. (1995). *Constructing the self, constructing America: A cultural history of psychotherapy*. Reading, MA: Addison-Wesley.
DeFehr, J., Adan, O., Barros, C., Rodriguez, S., & Wai, S. B. (2012). 'Not-knowing' and 'Assumption' in Canadian social services for refugees and immigrants: A conversational inquiry into practitioner stance. *International Journal of Collaborative Practices, 3*(1), 75–88.
Derrida, J. (1999). *Adieu: To Emmanuel Levinas*. Stanford, CA: Stanford University Press.
Duncan, B. L., Miller, S. D., Wampold, B. E., & Hubble, M. A. (Eds.). (2010). *The heart and soul of change: Delivering what works in therapy* (2nd ed.). Washington DC: American Psychological Association.
Epston, D. (2011). More travels with Herodotus: Tripping over borders lightly or "psychiatric imperialism". *Journal of Systemic Therapies, 30*(3), 1–11.
Foucault, M. (1980). *Power/Knowledge: Selected interviews and other writings, 1972–1977*. New York, NY: Pantheon Books.
Foucault, M. (2006). *Psychiatric power: Lectures at the College de France, 1973–1974*. (J. Lagrange Ed. G. Burchell Trans.). New York, NY: Picador.
Freedman, J., & Combs, G. (1996). *Narrative therapy: The social construction of preferred realities*. New York, NY: Norton.
Freeman, M. (2014). *The priority of the other: Thinking and living beyond the self*. Oxford, UK: Oxford University Press.
Gergen, K. (1998). Foreward. In M. F. Hoyt (Ed.), *The handbook of constructive therapies: Innovative approaches from leading practitioners*. San Francisco, CA: Jossey-Bass Publishers.
Gergen, K. (2009). *Relational being: Beyond self and community*. Oxford, England: Oxford University Press.
Hare-Mustin, R. T. (1994). Discourses in the mirrored room: A postmodern analysis of therapy. *Family Process, 33*(1), 19–35.
Harre, R. (1984). *Personal being: A theory for individual psychology*. Cambridge, MA: Harvard University Press.
Jenkins, A. (1990). *Invitation to responsibility: The therapeutic engagement of men who are violent and abusive*. Adelaide, AU: Dulwich Centre Publications.
Kapuscinski, R. (2008). *The other*. London, UK: Verso Books.
Laing, R. D. (1967). *The politics of experience*. New York, NY: Ballantine Books.
Larner, G. (2004). Levinas: Therapy as discourse ethics. In T. Strong & D. Pare (Eds), *Furthering talk: Advances in the discursive therapies*. New York, Boston, Dordrecht, London & Moscow: Kluver Academic/Plenum Publishers.
Levinas, E. (1987). *Time and the other*. (R. A. Cohen Trans.). Pittsburgh, PA: Duquesne University Press.
Levinas, E. (1993). *Outside the subject*. (M. B. Smith Trans.). Stanford, CA: Stanford University Press.
Levinas, E. (1995). Ethincs of the finite. In R. Kearney (Ed.), *States of mind: Dialogues with contemporary thinkers*. New York: New York University Press.

Levinas, E. (2001). In J. Robins (Ed.), *Interviews with Emmanuel Levinas*. Standford, CA: Stanford University Press.
Lock, A., & Strong, T. (2010). *Social constructionism: Sources and stirrings in theory and practice*. Cambridge, UK: Cambridge University Press.
Lomas, P. (1999). *Doing good? Psychotherapy out of its depth*. Oxford, UK: Oxford University Press.
Marmur, D. (2002). Ethical reflections on social inclusion. *Working papers series*. Toronto, Canada: Laidlaw Foundation.
Martin-Baro, I. (1994). *Writings for a liberation psychology*. Cambridge, MA: Harvard University Press.
Maturana, H., & Varela, F. (1987/1992). *The tree of knowledge: The biological roots of human understanding*. Boston, MA: Shambhala.
McCarthy, I. (1995). A spell in the fifth province: It's between myself, herself, yourself and your two imaginary friends. In S. Friedman (Ed.), *The reflecting team in action*. New York, NY: Guilford Press.
McCarthy, I. (2000). The fifth province approach—A realm of imagination and hopefulness. *Family therapy: The field's past, present and possible futures* (pp. 24–26). Adelaide AU: Dulwich Centre Publications.
McCarthy, I. (2004). The fifth province and spirituality: Co-creating a sacred space of love in therapy conversations. In S. Madigan (Ed.), *Therapeutic conversations 5: Therapy from the outside in* (pp. 1–16). Vancouver, Canada: Yaletown Family Therapy.
McCarthy, I. (2010). The fifth province: Imagining a space of dialogical co-creations. *Context*, (December), pp. 6–11.
McNamee, S. (2015). Radical presence: Alternatives to the therapeutic state (in press). *European Journal of Psychotherapy & Counselling, 17*(4), 373–383.
McNamee, S., & Hosking, D. M. (2012). *Research and social change: A relational constructionist approach*. New York, NY: Routledge.
Mental Health Commission of Canada. (2014). *Vancouver final report: At Home/Chez Soi project*. Retrieved from http://www.mentalhealthcommission.ca
Merton, T. (2001). *Dialogues with silence*. New York, NY: HarperCollins Publishers.
Myerhoff, B. (1982). Life history among the elderly: Performance, visibility and re-membering. In J. Ruby (Ed.), *A crack in the mirror: Reflexive perspectives in anthropology* (pp. 99–117). Philadelphia: University of Pennsylvania Press.
Robinson, M. (1990). Inaugural speech. Retrieved https://prelectur.standord.edu/lecturers/robinson/inaugural.html
Sampson, E. E. (1991). *Celebrating the other*. (Reprint). Chagrin Falls, OH: Taos Institute.
Sanders, C. (1996). Re-authoring problem identities: A postmodern inquiry. In C. Smith & D. Nylund (Eds.), *Narrative therapies with children and adolescents* (pp. 400–422). New York, NY: Guilford Press.
Sanders, C. (1998). Substance misuse dilemmas: A postmodern inquiry. In S. Madigan & I. Law (Eds.), *Praxis: Situating discourse, feminism, and politics in narrative therapies* (pp. 141–162). Vancouver, Canada: Yaletown Family Therapy/Cardigan Press.
Sanders, C. (2007). A poetics of resistance: Compassionate practice in substance misuse therapy. In C. Brown & T. Augusta-Scott (Eds.), *Narrative therapy: Making meaning, making lives* (pp. 59–76). Thousand Oaks, CA: Sage.
Sanders, C. J. (2010). News bulletin: An inside update on current government initiatives for the homeless and mentally ill. *Insights into Clinical Counselling, 40*, 16–18.
Sanders, C. J. (2012). The use of narrative therapy in the personal transformation of graduate students. *Insights into Counselling*, 22–23.
Sanders, C. J. (2013). An exploration of therapeutic practice as sacred engagement. *Insights into Counselling*, 16–17.
Sanders, C. J. (2014). Narrative poetics of resistance: Towards an aesthetics of engagement. http://www.taosinstitute.net/Websites/taos/images/PhDProgramCurrentDissertations/Sanders_Dissertation_2014_(2)-1.pdf

Sanders, C. J. (2015). Alan Watts: The contemporary relevance of *Psychotherapy east and west.* Manuscript in preparation.
Scott, C. (2014). Buberian dialogue as an intersubjective contemplative praxis. In O. Gunnlaugson, E. W. Sarath, C. Scott, & H. Bai (Eds.), *Contemplative learning and inquiry across disciplines.* Albany, NY: SUNY.
Seikula, J. (2002). Open dialogues with good and poor outcomes for psychotic crisis: Examples from families with violence. *Journal for Marital and Family Therapy, 28*(30), 263–274.
Seikula, J. (2011). Becoming dialogical: Psychotherapy or a way of life? *The Australian and New Zealand Journal of Family Therapy, 32*(3), 1769–1793.
Seikula, J., & Trimble, D. (2005). Healing elements of therapeutic conversation: Dialogue as an embodiment of love. *Family Process, 44*(4), 461–475.
Shotter, J. (2015). Tom Andersen, fleeting events, the bodily feelings they arouse in us, and the dialogical: Transitory understandings and action guiding implications. *Australian and New Zealand Journal of Family Therapy, 36*, 72–87.
Strong, T., & Pare, D. (Eds.). (2004). *Furthering talk: Advances in the discursive therapies.* New York, NY: Kluwer Academic/Plenum Publishers.
Szasz, T. (2007). *The medicalization of everyday life: Selected essays.* Syracuse, NY: Syracuse University Press.
Tomm, K. (1990). *A critique of the DSM* (Vol. 3, pp. 5–8). Adelaide: Dulwich Centre Newsletter.
Tomm, K. (1991). Beginnings of a "HIPS and PIPS" approach to psychiatric assessment. *The Calgary Participator*, 21–24.
Tomm, K. (1993). The courage to protest: A commentary on Michael White's work. In S. Gilligan & R. Price (Eds.), *Therapeutic conversations.* New York, NY: Norton.
Waldegrave, C., Tamasese, K., Tuhuka, F., & Campbell, W. (2003). *Just therapy—A journey: A collection of papers from the just therapy team, New Zealand.* Adelaide, AU: Dulwich Centre Publications.
White, M. (1991). *Deconstruction and therapy* (Vol. 2). Adelaide: Dulwich Centre Newsletter.
White, M. (1997). *Narratives of therapist's lives.* Adelaide AU: Dulwich Centre Publications.
White, M. (2011). *Narrative practices: Continuing the conversation.* New York, NY: Norton.
White, M. (2012). Scaffolding a therapeutic conversation. In T. Malinen, S. J. Cooper & F. N. Thomas (Eds.), *Masters of narrative and collaborative therapies: The voices of Andersen, Anderson, and White.* New York & London: Routledge.
White, M., & Epston, D. (1990). *Narrative means to therapeutic ends.* New York, NY: Norton.
Williams, B., & Baumgartner, B. (2014). Standing on the shoulder of giants: Narrative practices in support of frontline community work with homelessness, mental health, and substance use. *International Journal of Child, Youth & Family Studies, 5*(2), 240–257.
Wittgenstein, L. (2009). *Philosophical investigations*, (4th edn) (G. E. M. Anscombe, P. M. S. Hacker & J. Schulte Trans.). Oxford, UK: Oxford University Press.
Yukich, R., & Hoskins, T. K. (2011). Responsibility and the other: Cross-cultural engagement in the narratives of three New Zealand school leaders. *Journal of Systemic Therapies, 30*(3), 57–72.

# How Narrative Therapy Principles Inform Practice for Therapists and Helping Professionals: Illustrated with Vignettes

**John R. Stillman**

**Abstract** This chapter is intended for readers who do not yet practice narrative therapy or identify as narrative therapists. It organizes narrative therapy as a set of principles and focuses on helping practitioners move narrative principles into practice. This exploration of principles as a framework for narrative therapy is illustrated by the use of vignettes, which show the benefit of organizing narrative as principles for practitioners with various levels of experience and different practice areas as well as for a recently developed online training program. Principles discussed include narrative metaphor, positioning (de-centered, but influential; externalization), personal agency, subordinate story development (repositioning; absent but implicit), intentionality, identity proclamation, and deconstruction (societal and cultural; personal, day-to-day).

## Narrative Therapy Principles

In my roles as therapist, training director, and researcher, I believe that utilizing narrative therapy principles can respect the abilities of people to discern what they want in their lives. I hope that practitioners reading this chapter will learn how using narrative principles can empower people to live according to their values, allow focus beyond the individual, and recognize the impact of relationships, society, and culture on people's lives. Narrative therapy principles can guide clinicians' questions, awakening what people desire and reducing the impact of problems.

Viewing narrative therapy as a set of principles is a way of organizing the ideas created by White and Epston (1990) as well as leaving "space" for many other therapists, scholars, and researchers who have contributed to narrative and those that will contribute in the future. Narrative therapy principles help practitioners (1) capture and hold the ideas that inform narrative, keeping the principles visible over the course of a therapeutic conversation, (2) form possible questions within a conversation rather

J.R. Stillman (✉)
Caspersen Therapy and Training Center, St. Louis Park, MN, USA
e-mail: jstillman@visi.com

 
V. Dickerson (ed.), *Poststructural and Narrative Thinking in Family Therapy*,
AFTA SpringerBriefs in Family Therapy, DOI 10.1007/978-3-319-31490-7_6

than telling them specific questions to ask, and (3) use the narrative metaphor in their work, notice and ask about alternative stories to the dominant ones, and explore the concepts of personal agency, intentionality, and power. Also, organizing narrative therapy through principles allows narrative to be defined and even measured while also keeping the preference and style of the interviewer flexible. In addition, a focus on principles, versus specific practices, allows therapists and practitioners to explore other therapeutic approaches through a narrative lens.

Each narrative principle is supported by post-structural theory as well as many other theoretical underpinnings of narrative. Organizing narrative as a set of principles allows direct references to ideas from philosophy, anthropology, literature, feminist thought, and psychology, which inform the principles. In turn, the principles can influence practice. Also, as more ideas influence narrative, more principles can be formed and practices created that demonstrate the new principles. Principles both honor the work already established while also allowing narrative to grow and develop.

It is important to emphasize that the theoretical ideas that inform the principles do acknowledge the influence of society and culture on how people make meaning of their lives. Of equal importance is the influence of cultural norms within the conversations between practitioners and individuals. The practitioners' awareness of the potential impact of cultural norms influences their questions as they actively seek to expose and address how the norms influence people's descriptions of meaning. This emphasis on societal and cultural norms and the construction of meaning is explicitly stated within the principle of deconstruction (societal and cultural), and it is important to highlight because it is a key to narrative therapy.

The intended audience for this chapter is clinicians from multiple fields, including psychotherapists, social workers, nurses, and clergy who are curious about narrative therapy and how it might be useful in their work. There is an emphasis on the principles and how they might apply to practice, with a brief reference to the theories that supports them. For additional reading on narrative theory, principles, and practice, see References and References for Principles at the end of this chapter.

The principles discussed in this chapter represent narrative therapy as a respectful approach to practice. (See Glossary for more information about each principle.) They include the following:

- **Narrative Metaphor**: People make meaning of events in their lives through story.
- **Positioning (De-centered, but Influential), Personal Agency**: The person is the "expert" and respects the person's ability to make decisions for his or her own life.
- **Positioning (Externalization), Subordinate Story Development (Repositioning; Absent but Implicit)**: People are separate from the problems they face and can identify what they prefer.
- **Intentionality**: People's preferred stories are strengthened as they connect them to their preferred experiences and meaning in life.

- **Identity Proclamation, Deconstruction (Societal and Cultural; Personal, Day-to-Day)**: People's preferred stories are further supported as they connect to their relationships, viewed in the context of their cultural framework, and explored in their day-to-day routines.

Note that the narrative principles discussed in this chapter do not represent all the principles that inform narrative therapy. I take full responsibility for the selection of the specific principles and their presentation, but at the same time, I do not claim authorship because there are many people, in addition to White and Epston (1990), who have contributed to the ideas of these principles. (See References for Principles in reference list.)

## Narrative Principles Illustrated with Vignettes

The exploration of using principles as a framework for organizing narrative is illustrated in this chapter by the use of vignettes. The first seven vignettes demonstrate how narrative therapy can be used by professionals (and those in training) with different specialties and various levels of experience in their fields. The final vignette illustrates how the structure of an online, on-site training program can be organized and modeled according to narrative principles. I hope that practitioners who have not considered using narrative therapy in the past will be encouraged to use it in their future work with clients and in teaching.

The vignettes are composites of feedback I received from practitioners in fifteen years. They purposefully do not refer to any one person. By creating each vignette as representative of several professional accounts and experiences, I was free to add dimensions to the conversation and commentary without the need to protect a particular person's position and story. In addition, by using vignettes, the chapter is written in a style that supports the principles. For example, I and the chapter itself are "de-centered, but influential," allowing readers to be an audience to stories, so they can choose what resonates for them. References to the principles listed in the titles of the vignettes are presented at the end of the chapter and not within the vignettes themselves to enhance the reading experience.

## Vignettes

### *Vignette #1: Student—Positioning (De-centered, but Influential), Positioning (Externalization), Deconstruction (Societal), Identity Proclamation*

Sarah is a master's student, studying for her licensure in marriage and family therapy. She has known for a long time that she likes helping people, so she decided becoming a marriage and family therapist would be the best way to express her passion and values. She is enjoying both her classroom and practicum experiences, and even though there have been small bumps along the way, she feels good about her decision.

Sarah's program exposed her to several different therapeutic approaches, and she must now identify which approach to focus on. This is a difficult decision for Sarah because, ideally, she would like to take a bit from all of the therapies she has studied, but she understands why she must focus on a specific therapeutic approach. Sarah's criteria for choosing a specific approach include the following: First, she wants to have a concrete set of tools that will help her on the job. Because Sarah is understandably anxious about starting her career, she thinks using a model with well-defined, clear steps will ease interactions with people. Second, she wants to practice a well-known, widely used, evidence-based approach. Finally, she wants an approach that fits with her values of how she wants to interact with people, how she views the people with whom she works, and how she understands change happens in people's lives. In addition, she prefers an approach that will incorporate social justice and feminism, ideas she considers very important in her work and life.

After much thought, Sarah chose a well-established, evidence-based therapeutic approach that provides clear directions for working with people and is cited frequently in academic journals. She completed the necessary forms and was ready to proceed with the program. But then she discovered narrative therapy. Narrative therapy was clearly not as strongly established as other therapeutic approaches. However, Sarah was encouraged when learning that there is some promising research supporting narrative therapy, although not enough to label it evidence-based (Erbes et al. 2014). Also, narrative therapy did not propose clear, concrete steps to take when meeting with people. Actually, it seemed somewhat "soft" to Sarah and challenged some of the ways she had been taught. So why was she considering focusing on it as her main approach? The answer for Sarah was that narrative therapy's principles align with the values that attracted her to becoming a therapist, and in addition, the principles fit the way she wants to interact with people and what she views as the best avenue to help. Also, she could see how her passion for social justice and feminism influenced narrative principles and would help guide her work.

Sarah eventually chose to pursue narrative therapy as her focus. Although she experiences anxiety because narrative therapy does not give clear directions, she does appreciate the trade-off that its principles inform possible questions. She also respects that narrative therapy allows the person to direct the session and be the expert, while her job is to ask questions, informed by narrative principles, that will help the person identify problems and what he or she would prefer instead (de-centered, but influential). She likes that separating the person from the problem sets up a collaborative relationship of discovery (externalization). Sarah is learning how to ask questions that challenge societal norms (deconstruction) and how to encourage other stakeholders to be part of the work either directly or indirectly (identity proclamation).

At first, she thought separating the person from the problem meant that people had to solve their own problems, and the therapist was not actively involved or helpful, but now knows this is not true. Sarah is also continually surprised by all the dimensions of narrative therapy, rooted in ideas from philosophy, literature, psychology, and feminist thought. While narrative therapy is not as concrete as she would like (telling her exactly what to do), she likes that the principles themselves inform possible questions centered on the direction set by the person. This fits with how she wants to interact with people in her work. The principles also allow her to weave in aspects of other approaches that she enjoyed learning in school. This appeals to Sarah because instead of viewing therapeutic approaches as separate silos that do not interact, narrative therapy provides an overarching paradigm within which she can use tools of other therapeutic practices. Sarah feels good about her choice.

## *Vignette #2: Newly Licensed Professional Clinical Counselor (LPCC)—Subordinate Story Development (Repositioning), Intentionality, Positioning (Externalization), Identity Proclamation, Positioning (De-centered, but Influential)*

Marsha had just earned her LPCC license and started work at an agency, seeing clients individually as well as families and couples. Marsha's supervisor gave very clear direction when Marsha consulted with her about a case. This direction was helpful when Marsha was new at the job, but she sometimes found that her supervisor's advice did not work with her client. However, when the sessions went well with Marsha emulating and using her supervisor's directive style, clients started depending on her to help them figure out their next steps. At first, Marsha liked this because she saw her clients' reliance as doing her job, but after a while, it became too much as her clients called her at all times. When she could not meet her clients' needs, they were disappointed, and so was Marsha.

Then, her supervisor went on vacation for two weeks, and Marsha faced some challenging clients. She discovered she needed her supervisor as much as her clients needed her. So Marsha thought of the previous consults with her supervisor that might apply to her clients' present issues and tried to piece together what her supervisor would suggest, but that process did not work well. After some time, she reviewed her notes from her education, looking for other ways that might be helpful. She came across narrative therapy. She had liked this approach when learning about it in school, but it seemed so different from other therapies that she paid little attention to it. However, when reviewing her notes, she was intrigued by the idea of principles informing practice. The principles did not necessarily tell her *what* to do, but instead gave her a framework of how to present questions to clients. For example, Marsha read about the principle of repositioning that suggests when a person experiences a time or situation when the problem is less present, this exception can become the focus of the conversation. The exception can then gain strength by being connected to and woven into the story about what the person identifies as preferring in life (intentionality). Even though Marsha was still unclear about the principle of repositioning, she started thinking about a client, a family that was dealing with a lot of stress. She recalled that there were times in their day that family members identified as less stressful and different places or experiences where they felt almost free of stress. At their next meeting, Marsha reviewed these times and places with the family and learned more about what supported the "free-from-stressing-out" periods (externalization). She encouraged them to work on expanding those times and also use their newly identified supports to help during the stressful times (identity proclamation).

Now Marsha has a different idea of what "direction" means, and she has a new supervisor, one who asks her questions and respects her ability to determine whether the advice will work for her client. Marsha now approaches her clients in the same way, making sure to keep their viewpoints at the center of the conversations. While she is still active in the sessions, she insures that her clients are the ones directing the sessions (de-centered, but influential).

## *Vignette #3: Experienced Marriage and Family Therapist—Positioning (De-centered, but Influential), Positioning (Externalization)*

Phil is a marriage and family therapist and has been in practice for 15 years. He identifies as an eclectic therapist but mostly uses a well-known approach that gives him a focus and direction in his work. Over the years, he has been exposed to narrative therapy but did not think it would benefit his practice. However, Phil recently attended a workshop where the presenter spoke about narrative as a set of principles and said that although these principles inform questions that are associated with narrative therapy, they are also inclusive of practices that are informed by other therapy traditions as well. The presenter addressed this specifically by saying that "narrative can play well with others," meaning that a conversation about principles (versus practices) allows for more collaboration among different therapeutic approaches. For example, Phil likes the principles—the client being the expert and that people are separated from problems—and can envision using those principles successfully in his practice (de-centered, but influential; externalization). It will take a bit of work on his part, though, because he has traditionally held the views that the therapist is the expert and the problems are internal to the person. However, Phil thinks his effort to incorporate narrative therapy principles into his therapeutic approach will be rewarded and show that narrative indeed does "play well with others." Phil is now energized and enthusiastic about learning about other narrative principles that he can bring into his work.

## *Vignette #4: Experienced Psychologist—Personal Agency, Narrative Metaphor, Identity Proclamation, Deconstruction (Personal, Day-to-Day; Societal and Cultural)*

Jane, a psychologist in practice for 20 years, identifies herself as a narrative therapist. Two years ago, Jane was introduced to the idea that narrative can be studied as a set of principles. She respects that narrative has many dimensions and referring to narrative in terms of principles allows a way to talk about different components of it. She also found that the principles were broad enough to encompass the work being done within narrative therapy by many people while also being specific enough to identify practices that were influenced by the principles. She is also drawn to narrative because it respects her clients' abilities to make decisions for their own lives (personal agency). It also makes sense to her that people actively seek understanding of events in their lives and they organize these events by developing a story. The narrative metaphor, composed of actions, in a sequence across time and according to a plot, provides many avenues in her conversations with people and the problems they face. She also finds narrative to be very innovative and most important, it openly addresses the issues of power within relationships, communities, society, and culture. She likes how the therapy does not focus solely on the individual, but includes the effects of both the clients' relationships with others and societal and cultural norms (identity proclamation; deconstruction).

Jane has recently been exploring additional approaches. She is interested in eye movement desensitization and reprocessing (EMDR) treatment (Shapiro 2001) and acceptance and commitment therapy (ACT) (Hayes 2005) and has found that narrative principles can serve as an umbrella or a frame of reference when using these approaches.

While Jane is convinced herself that narrative is an effective approach, she also understands why evidence-based approaches have more credibility in the psychological community. However, she is encouraged that initial research using narrative principles with veterans who are struggling with PTSD has shown promising results (Erbes et al. 2014).

## *Vignette #5: County Social Worker—Positioning (De-centered, but Influential), Personal Agency, Identity Proclamation*

Mark, a county case manager, with ten years of experience and a master's in social work, likes his job but sometimes finds it very challenging. He routinely follows up with his clients, supporting them with basic and essential housing and medical needs. Clear and obtainable goal setting is an important aspect of his work with clients, but this can be challenging because their motivation levels and complexity of their problems often impede their progress. When a colleague introduced narrative therapy to him, his first thoughts were, "How would that pertain to me? First, I only meet with people for a short time to help them form concrete goals. Second, many of the people I work with have lower intellectual functioning, so talk therapy about the meaning of their lives is not going to be effective." Although he was skeptical, Mark attended a narrative therapy workshop and was pleased to learn that narrative therapy principles could enhance his work with clients. For example, he found that the principles of positioning and personal agency could positively affect his practice. When working with his clientele, Mark found it easy to take on the "expert" role and be directive and assertive, while hoping that his behavior came across as positive encouragement. When he considered "positioning" the clients as the experts and supporting their "personal agency," his initial reaction was to balk and say that it would not work, but he tried it anyway. Although having the clients be the experts did not always work, Mark saw improvement in their progress because their opinions were sought and they were credited more with their decisions. Any deviations from their goals were not seen as failures, but as opportunities to redefine their plans to fit with what they, the clients, wanted to pursue. Sometimes this meant that the goals were not as lofty as Mark preferred, but he discovered that smaller goals sometimes aligned more with clients' motivations and over time these smaller goals amounted to more than the bigger goals. He still directed and encouraged his clients, but liked the new positioning of the clients being the expert and he influential but de-centered.

Mark also appreciates that relationships are a main focus of narrative. He learned at the workshop that people do not create their identity in a vacuum, but rather it is co-constructed with others. This relates to his clients in a very direct way because often family members are very involved in his clients' care and relating to family members and their positions adds a level of complexity to Mark's already challenging work. He has found the narrative principle, identity proclamation, opens up space in conversation for different positions among family members to be very helpful. Rather than seeing the family members' relationships with him as conflictive, Mark now views these relationships as assets, although challenging at times. Also, using the specific practice, the outsider witness map (White 2007), has given Mark a way to facilitate conversations with relatives.

Mark was grateful to be introduced to narrative because he found its principles applied to case management. However, he wonders why it is named "narrative therapy" as the name implies that it is just for therapists and thinks if it were called something else, more people would be inclined to learn about it and use it help their clients.

## *Vignette #6: Clergy—Narrative Metaphor, Subordinate Story Development (Repositioning, Absent but Implicit), Personal Agency, Intentionality*

Joseph is a priest and counsels parishioners on a wide array of issues and is passionate about helping people sort out problems in their lives. Because Joseph came to counseling through the ministry and not psychology, he feels less constrained to use a particular therapy and instead choose an approach that fits best for the person. He was introduced to narrative therapy several years ago. He likes it primarily because it is directed by the person, allowing him and the parishioner to explore together stories that hold meaning in the person's life (narrative metaphor). Joseph also appreciates that while a person describes a problem, he can ask them about times when the problem did not have as much influence, and if the problem was having a large effect on the parishioner's life, he could ask what it was affecting. Both of these principles (repositioning and the absent but implicit) allow Joseph to remain present with the person while they describe the problem and ask questions about what could help the person develop what he or she wants instead. What is so exciting for Joseph is that *he* does not need to create these exceptions, but that he respects people's abilities to identify and determine both the times when the problem was not as bad and what they would rather be doing (personal agency). They can also speak to how the problem takes them away from what they value and then talk about those values (absent but implicit, intentionality). Joseph connects this process to spirituality but realizes that not everyone practicing narrative therapy would do so. However, for Joseph, narrative therapy fits nicely with his spiritual practices and how God works in people's lives.

## *Vignette #7: Nurse—Positioning (De-centered, but Influential), Positioning (Externalization)*

Sally is a nurse on a hospital inpatient unit serving children who are being treated for cancer. Being on the oncology floor gives her opportunities to get to know her patients over a longer period than normal because the children come for treatments and many times return when the cancer flares. Sally's job is to perform basic nursing tasks, which requires a bit of finesse with children, and she relies on the relationships she builds with them in the moment to do her job well. Although Sally is not a therapist or social worker, the people she works with do not differentiate such roles. The child and family often look to her for comfort, and although she can make a referral, it is often late at night when people need to talk, and all of the therapists and social workers have gone home. Sally has to balance these conversations with the requirements of her job, but it is these connections with her patients that bring her the most meaning.

When Sally told a clinical nurse specialist that she wished she had basic tools to help guide interactions with patients and their families, the specialist suggested that narrative principles could be helpful. In fact, the specialist said narrative principles influence her own patient care work. The specialist explained the two aspects of positioning—de-centered, but influential and externalization: She asked Sally to imagine a triangle with point one representing the patient; point two, the nurse; and point three, the "effects of cancer." The line between the patient and nurse illustrates the de-centered, but influential idea, meaning that although the nurse has influence, the patient is the expert. The line from the nurse to the effects of cancer shows that it is the job of the nurse (and the overall medical establishment) to equip the patient with the best knowledge to make decisions for his or her health. Finally, the line from the patient to the effects of cancer represents the respect given to the patient to choose the best course for care. Positioning herself as de-centered, but influential, has positively affected Sally's interactions with patients because they no longer view her as being in charge, but instead, they are making the decisions. She also finds that having the external reference point, in this case, "the effects of cancer," to be helpful because she and the patient refer to the effects as outside of the patient, thus positioning Sally and the patient as a team. This helps Sally balance the requirements of her nurse role but also still have meaningful interactions with patients and families. Using narrative principles has transformed how Sally performs patient care.

## *Vignette #8: Certificate Program Attendee—Positioning (De-centered, but Influential), Identity Proclamation*

Joe is attending Caspersen Therapy and Training Center's nine-month narrative therapy certificate program. The program focuses on teaching narrative as a set of principles with presentations by well-known narrative teachers. The program features monthly workshops over nine months along with seven months of small group practice. The workshops demonstrate the many ways that narrative can be applied when working with different populations—children and families, couples, and young adults—and also to specific problem areas such as drug and alcohol addiction, nightmares, and trauma, along with how narrative relates to broader areas such as neurology, dialectical behavior therapy (DBT) (Linehan 1993), and acceptance and commitment therapy (ACT) (Hayes 2005). Joe appreciates that after attending these workshops, he will have not only a thicker idea of narrative itself but also how it relates to other ideas and practices. While Joe attends on-site in Minnesota, the workshop teachers present their sessions from their own state or country, and Joe is able to view and interact with them as well as with the online participants attending from around the world. Joe especially likes how the role of the facilitator is structured in the workshops. When an attendee asks a question, and before the speaker responds, the facilitator (who is often the training director) will ask the questioner a few more questions about what he or she is thinking. This thickens the conversation so that the speaker gets a more substantial question and more time to think about the response. Joe understands this process as keeping the speaker de-centered, but influential, an important positioning principle in narrative. It also allows the questioner to explore further how the question being discussed resonates and fits with his or her experiences and social context. This shift of the facilitator and speaker to being an audience to the questioner thickens and enriches the conversation. This practice in a workshop context supports identity proclamation, another narrative principle, and leads to thick story development.

In the small groups, attendees also participate online and on-site. This experience allows for small numbers of people to discuss and practice the ideas. Joe especially likes this component of the program because he meets people from around the world and learns from their different cultural and societal experiences. The reading and writing assignments help Joe integrate the theory that informs narrative into his day-to-day practice. The narrative principles, in particular, give him a bridge between the two, so he gains a framework that will help him hold on to narrative ideas and inform his future practice. The certificate program is not only enriching his daily practice of the ideas but also helping him to establish a community of people from around the world who have similar interests in their practices and their lives. Joe hopes to stay in contact with his friends from around the globe and maybe even visit them one day.

## Conclusion

These vignettes demonstrate how professionals with various licenses and experience levels can be influenced by narrative principles. They also show that narrative has uses outside of individual therapy and can be helpful to those in nursing, ministry, and social work. This project could also lead to further works which would use vignettes to show how narrative is used with different compositions of people, from individuals and families, to couples and groups, and how it can be useful with specific problems. The vignette format is meant to be a tangible way that readers can see narrative principles demonstrated and envision using them in their own practice. See Stillman (2010) for more information and details about the narrative principles discussed in this chapter.

## Glossary

**Deconstruction (Personal, Day-to-Day)** People's day-to-day activities can support problems and impact their ability to live their preferred lives. Routines can have an impact at a physical level. The practitioner can ask questions that help the person identify the effects of day-to-day routines, so the person is in a position to take action.

| | |
|---|---|
| **Deconstruction (Societal and Cultural)** | People's identities and experiences are shaped by society and culture. Often taken for granted as assumptions, society and culture's meanings and norms influence people in ways that they are aware of and in ways they are not. These meanings and norms can both support problems or help a person stand up to problems. The clinician can ask questions that identify and expose these meanings and norms so that the person can take an active position regarding them. This awareness influences actions that help the person develop his or her preferred ways of living. |
| **Identity Proclamation** | People do not live in vacuums; their identities are influenced by their relationships to others. Relationships can both support the problem and/or support people to claim what they desire. Practitioners can ask questions that expose these relationships, allowing people to either decrease the influence of those voices that support problems or magnify voices that support what they prefer. |
| **Intentionality** | People's identities are made of events and meanings that are acquired through experience and relationships and within a cultural context. Exceptions to problems can be supported and strengthened by asking questions that connect them to the person's identity. The resulting effect is the diminishing influence of the problem stories. |
| **Narrative Metaphor** | People make meaning of events in their lives through story. The stories they tell impact how they view their past, present, and future. These stories can be reauthored to become preferred stories, using the components that comprise a story, such as action, time, sequence, plot, context, relationships, and cultural and societal influence. |

| | |
|---|---|
| **Personal Agency** | The practitioner respects the person's ability to make life decisions, determining what is a problem and what is desired. The practitioner actively seeks and tracks these determinations and presents them back to the person, while the person discusses their past, present, and future. |
| **Positioning (De-centered, but Influential**) | The person is the expert, not the practitioner. Curiosity defines the person–practitioner relationship as the practitioner actively inquires about how the person makes meaning of his or her life. The interviewer is active, not passive, about attending to what the person defines as preferred and asks questions that help identify how problems interfere with the person's life. |
| **Positioning (Externalization)** | People are not seen as the problem; the problem is seen as the problem. The separation of the problem from the person allows for a relational shift from the practitioner working *on* the person to the practitioner working *with* the person to address the effects of the problem. Externalization is not limited to problems but can include discussing desires in the same way. It also allows the practitioner to bring ideas into the conversation without ownership. This results in a more equitable power relationship between the clinician and the person, letting the person choose the ideas or not. |
| **Subordinate Story Development (Absent but Implicit)** | Every problem has its implied opposite. Another way to express this is that a problem is defined as a problem because there is knowledge of something that the person would rather have in its place. A person can be asked about what the problem is interfering with and speak to what they prefer and desire instead. |
| **Subordinate Story Development (Repositioning)** | All stories have exceptions. As a person recounts a problem story, there are typically instances when the problem did not occur or when the degree of the problem was reduced. The influential clinician listens to and asks for these alternative stories as they often lead to a description of what the person desires and experiences when possible. |

## References

Erbes, C. R., Stillman, J. R., Wieling, E., Bera, W., & Leskela, J. (2014). A pilot examination of the use of narrative therapy with individuals diagnosed with PTSD. *Journal of Traumatic Stress, 27*, 730–733.

Hayes, S. (2005). *Get out of your mind and into your life: The new acceptance and commitment therapy (a New Harbinger self-help workbook)*. Oakland, CA: New Harbinger.

Linehan, M. (1993). *Cognitive-behavioral treatment of borderline personality disorder*. New York, NY: Guilford Press.

Shapiro, F. (2001). *Eye movement desensitization and reprocessing (EMDR): Basic principles, protocols, and procedures* (2nd ed.). New York, NY: Guilford Press.

Stillman, J. (2010). *Narrative therapy trauma manual: A principle-based approach*. Minneapolis, MN: Caspersen.

White, M. (2007a). *Maps of narrative practice*. New York, NY: W. W. Norton.

White, M., & Epston, D. (1990a). *Narrative means to therapeutic ends*. New York, NY: W. W. Norton.

## References for Principles

**Principle: Narrative Metaphor**

Bruner, J. (1990). *Acts of meaning*. Cambridge, MA: Harvard University Press.

White, M. (1995). The narrative perspective in therapy. In M. White (Ed.), *Re-authoring lives: Interviews and essays* (pp. 11–40). Adelaide, Australia: Dulwich Centre Publications.

White, M., & Epston, D. (1990). *Narrative means to therapeutic ends*. New York, NY: W. W. Norton.

**Principle: Positioning—De-centered, but Influential**

White, M. (1997). *Narratives of therapists' lives*. Adelaide, Australia: Dulwich Centre Publications.

White, M. (2001). Folk psychology and narrative practice. *International Journal of Narrative Therapy and Community Work, 2*, 3–37.

White, M., & Epston, D. (1990). *Narrative means to therapeutic ends*. New York, NY: W. W. Norton.

**Principle: Positioning—Externalization**

White, M. (1991). Deconstruction and therapy. In D. Epston & M. White (Eds.), *Experience, contradiction, narrative, and imagination* (pp. 109–152). Adelaide, Australia: Dulwich Centre Publications.

White, M., & Epston, D. (1990). *Narrative means to therapeutic ends*. New York, NY: W. W. Norton.

**Principle: Personal Agency**

White, M. (2001). Folk psychology and narrative practice. *International Journal of Narrative Therapy and Community Work, 2*, 3–37.

White, M. (2003). *Michael White workshop notes*. Retrieved from http://www.dulwichcentre.com.au

White, M. (2007). *Maps of narrative practice*. New York, NY: W. W. Norton.

**Principle: Subordinate Story Development—Repositioning**

White, M. (2004). Working with people who are suffering the consequences of multiple trauma: A narrative perspective. *Dulwich Centre Journal, 1*, 45–76.

White, M. (2005). Children, trauma, and subordinate storyline development. *International Journal of Narrative Therapy and Community Work, 3–4*, 10–21.

**Principle: Subordinate Story Development—Absent but Implicit**
Carey, M., Walther, S., & Russell, S. (2009). The absent but implicit: A map to support therapeutic enquiry. *Family Process, 48*, 319–331.
Freedman, J. (2012). Explorations of the absent but implicit. *International Journal of Narrative Therapy and Community Work, 4*, 1–10.
White, M. (2000). Re-engaging with history: The absent but implicit. In M. White (Ed.), *Reflections on narrative practice: Essays and interviews* (pp. 35–58). Adelaide, Australia: Dulwich Centre Publications.
White, M. (2003). Narrative practice and community assignments. *International Journal of Narrative Therapy and Community Work, 2*, 17–55.
White, M. (2004). Working with people who are suffering the consequences of multiple trauma: A narrative perspective. *Dulwich Centre Journal, 1*, 45–76.
White, M. (2005). Children, trauma, and subordinate storyline development. *International Journal of Narrative Therapy and Community Work, 3–4*, 10–21.
**Principle: Intentionality**
White, M. (2001). Folk psychology and narrative practice. *International Journal of Narrative Therapy and Community Work, 2*, 3–37.
White, M. (2003). *Michael White workshop notes*. Retrieved from http://www.dulwichcentre.com.au
White, M. (2007). *Maps of narrative practice*. New York, NY: W. W. Norton.
**Principle: Identity Proclamation**
Anderson, T. (1987). The reflecting team: Dialogue and meta-dialogue in clinical work. *Family Process, 26*, 415–428.
Freeman, J., Epston, D., & Lobovits, D. (1997). *Playful approaches to serious problems*. New York, NY: W. W. Norton.
Myerhoff, B. (1982). Life history among the elderly: Performance, visibility, and remembering. In J. Ruby (Ed.), *A crack in the mirror: Reflective perspectives in anthropology* (pp. 99–117). Philadelphia, PA: University of Pennsylvania Press.
Myerhoff, B. (1986). Life not death in Venice: Its second life. In V. Turner & E. Bruner (Eds.), *The anthropology of experience* (pp. 261–286). Chicago, IL: University of Illinois Press.
White, M. (1995). The narrative perspective in therapy. In M. White (Ed.), *Re-authoring lives: Interviews and essays* (pp. 11–40). Adelaide, Australia: Dulwich Centre Publications.
White, M. (1995). Reflecting teamwork as definitional ceremony. In M. White (Ed.), *Re-authoring lives: Interviews and essays* (pp. 172–198). Adelaide, Australia: Dulwich Centre Publications.
White, M. (1995). Therapeutic documents revisited. In M. White (Ed.), *Re-authoring lives: Interviews and essays* (pp. 199–213). Adelaide, Australia: Dulwich Centre Publications.
White, M. (1997). *Narratives of therapists' lives*. Adelaide, Australia: Dulwich Centre Publications.
White, M. (2003). *Michael White workshop notes*. Retrieved from http://www.dulwichcentre.com.au
White, M. (2004). Working with people who are suffering the consequences of multiple trauma: A narrative perspective. *Dulwich Centre Journal, 1*, 45–76.
White, M. (2005). Children, trauma, and subordinate storyline development. *International Journal of Narrative Therapy and Community Work, 3–4*, 10–21.
White, M. (2007). *Maps of narrative practice*. New York, NY: W. W. Norton.
White, M., & Epston, D. (1990). *Narrative means to therapeutic ends*. New York, NY: W. W. Norton.
**Principle: Deconstruction—Societal and Cultural; Personal, Day-to-Day**
Freedman, J., & Combs, G. (1996). *Narrative therapy: The social construction of preferred realities*. New York, NY: W. W. Norton.
White, M. (1991). Deconstruction and therapy. In D. Epston & M. White (Eds.), *Experience, contradiction, narrative, and imagination* (pp. 109–152). Adelaide, Australia: Dulwich Centre Publications.
White, M. (2001). Narrative practice and the unpacking of identity conclusions. *Gecko: A Journal of Deconstruction and Narrative Ideas in Therapeutic Practice, 1*, 28–55.

MIX
Papier aus verantwortungsvollen Quellen
Paper from responsible sources
FSC® C105338

If you have any concerns about our products,
you can contact us on
**ProductSafety@springernature.com**

In case Publisher is established outside the EU,
the EU authorized representative is:
**Springer Nature Customer Service Center GmbH**
**Europaplatz 3, 69115 Heidelberg, Germany**

Printed by Libri Plureos GmbH
in Hamburg, Germany